EVOLUTION

Natural History Museum

EVOLUTION

JOIN US ON AN EXHILARATING JOURNEY FROM THE ORIGINS OF LIFE TO THE PRESENT DAY!

WRITTEN BY REAL-LIFE SCIENTISTS

SARAH DARWIN & EVA-MARIA SADOWSKI

ILLUSTRATED BY OLGA BAUMERT

What on Earth Books

CONTENTS

Introduction 6–7
Darwin and Wallace 8–9
Natural Selection 10–11
The Game of Life 12–13
How it all Began – Hadean and Archean Eons 14–15
Planet Earth Rocks! 16–17
Life Fills the Seas – Proterozoic Eon and Cambrian Period 18–19
Life Finds a New Home – Ordovician and Silurian Periods 20–21
Fantastic Fossils 22–23
Animals Find Their Feet – Devonian Period 24–25
Giants from the Swamps – Carboniferous Period 26–27
From Icehouse to Hothouse – Permian Period 28–29
The Causes of Climate Change 30–31
Dinosaurs in Charge – Triassic and Jurassic Periods 32–33
T. rex and the Rise of Flowers – Cretaceous Period 34–35

Evolving Together 36–37
The Age of Mammals – Palaeogene Period 38–39
Grasslands and Grazers – Neogene Period 40–41
The Success of Birds 42–43
Evolution of Humans – Neogene and Quaternary Periods 44–45
Humans Change Their World – Quaternary Period 46–47
Human-Made – Quaternary Period 48–49
The Future 50–51
The Tree of Life 52–53
World Map 54–55
Glossary 56–57
Index 58–59
Sources 60–61
Natural History Collections 62
Meet the Authors 63

BRILLIANT BIODIVERSITY

Our planet is teeming with life: it's crawling, running, flying, swimming, wafting and sometimes, just waiting. This variety of living things is known as biodiversity. About two million different species have been named by scientists so far. A species is a group of closely related living things whose members can have offspring together. Some scientists estimate that we only know about 10 per cent of the species that may exist today! This picture shows the Amazon rainforest in Brazil. The Amazon is home to tens of thousands of different species of plants, animals and fungi, and lots more that have yet to be discovered.

INTRODUCTION

Welcome to the story of evolution! Join us on a tour through Earth's history to see the events that shaped the natural world. Evolution is simply the way that living things change over time, often in order to suit their environment.

In this book we will explain how evolution works and introduce you to some of the amazing animals, plants and fungi that have lived on our planet. We can't wait to show you how plants conquered the land, how animals got their legs, why dinosaurs aren't really extinct and how lots of evolution took place for you to be able to chew your breakfast!

To help guide us on our journey, we have included a timeline along the bottom of some of the pages. This is the geological timeline, which is how we chart the time from the formation of Earth until now. The timeline is divided into different-sized chunks with different names.

Along the way we will be joined by many pioneering people who have helped unlock the mysteries of evolution. New discoveries are being made all the time, and we have done our best to share the most up-to-date scientific information with you. But scientists are constantly finding out new things, so this is not the end of the story...

Sarah & Eva

DARWIN AND WALLACE

For thousands of years, humans have wondered how Earth's amazing variety of life came to be. Many communities have told stories of creation to try to explain the natural world. In the mid 1800s, two men, Charles Darwin and Alfred Russel Wallace, came up with very similar suggestions to explain the extraordinary variety of living things in a scientific way. Their theory is called evolution by natural selection.

EARLY IDEAS

In the 1700s and 1800s, some naturalists (people who study the natural world) thought that living things could develop certain characteristics, or features, during their lifetimes. These characteristics would then be passed on to their young. This idea was known as transmutation of species and, while it was an interesting scientific idea, we now know it is not that simple.

The giraffe's neck is an example of how people imagined transmutation of species might work. If a giraffe stretched its neck throughout its life to reach leaves in the treetops, then its neck would become longer.

This longer neck would be inherited by its offspring who would pass it on to their offspring.

BIG ADVENTURES

Darwin and Wallace had lots in common: they were both British, enjoyed exploring nature and especially loved collecting beetles. They both dreamed of travelling to faraway places and each set off on separate journeys. Darwin voyaged around the world in the ship the HMS *Beagle* between 1831 and 1836. Wallace travelled around South America between 1848 and 1852, and Southeast Asia between 1854 and 1862.

HMS *Beagle*

ON THE SHOULDERS OF GIANTS

Darwin and Wallace carefully observed the world around them. But they also read lots of books and communicated with great thinkers of their time. Here, together with Darwin and Wallace, are a few of the people whose work or discoveries influenced them.

Ⓐ **Charles Darwin** (1809–1882) *left*, and **Alfred Russel Wallace** (1823–1913) *right*
Darwin and Wallace came up with the theory of evolution by natural selection at about the same time.

Ⓑ **John Stevens Henslow** (1796–1861)
Studied variation within plant species.

Ⓒ **Charles Lyell** (1797–1875)
Laid out the basic ideas of modern geology and showed that Earth was much older than many people had previously thought.

Ⓓ **Mary Anning** (1799–1847)
Discovered many fossils of extinct sea creatures, including the first Ichthyosaur fossil.

Ⓔ **John Herschel** (1792–1871)
Suggested a scientific method that included using observations to figure out how the world works.

Ⓕ **Georges Cuvier** (1769–1832)
Was a leader in the study of animals' bodies and proved that living things could go extinct.

Ⓖ **Jean-Baptiste Lamarck** (1744–1829)
Wrote about transmutation in his influential book *Philosophie Zoologique*.

Ⓗ **Alexander von Humboldt** (1769–1859) Looked at the natural world in a scientific way. His books inspired Darwin and Wallace to travel.

Ⓘ **Erasmus Darwin** (1731–1802)
Charles's grandfather, who wrote about evolution 70 years before Charles did. But Erasmus didn't know how evolution worked.

Ⓙ **Thomas Malthus** (1766–1834)
Suggested that an increase in the human population would mean food supplies might run out. Darwin and Wallace thought this might be the same for animals, too.

OBSERVATIONS

During their travels, Darwin and Wallace both became excited by the variety of living things that they found in each area. This started each of them thinking about how species might form and change over time. It was a gradual build-up of these observations and ideas that brought both Darwin and Wallace to their conclusions.

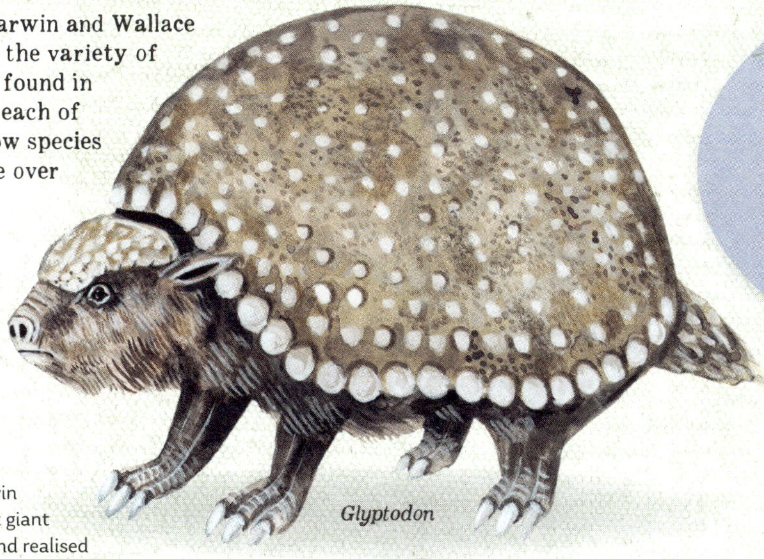

Glyptodon

Armadillo

Ancient relatives

While in South America, Darwin found fossil remains of extinct giant animals. He examined them and realised that they were similar to living animals. For example, he noticed that the fossil of the extinct *Glyptodon* looked similar to living armadillos. This made him think about how these creatures might be related.

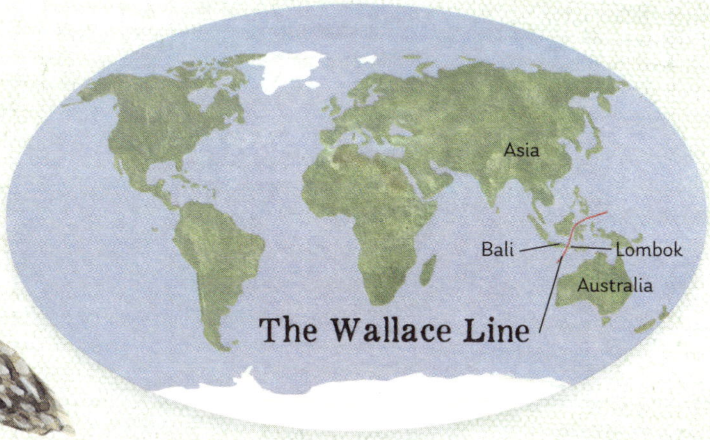

The Wallace Line

During his time in Asia, Wallace encountered a puzzle. He noticed that some of the animals in the western islands of what is now Indonesia, such as Bali, were very different to those found in the nearby eastern islands, such as Lombok. We now know that there is a deep ocean trench that runs between the islands that has kept these different animals separated from each other. Even when sea levels were lower, the deep trench still prevented the animals from crossing this boundary. This is called 'the Wallace Line', in his honour.

TWIN THEORIES

Darwin and Wallace independently came up with ideas to explain how evolution worked. After Darwin's world voyage he returned home and worked steadily on his theory for more than 20 years. Meanwhile, in Southeast Asia, Wallace came up with his own ideas and sent them to Darwin to get his opinion. Darwin was shocked to read that Wallace's theory was nearly identical to his own! Both men had come up with a concept called natural selection to explain how evolution works. Natural selection is a process that leads to evolution and the formation of new species.

The Linnean Society in Burlington House, London, in the mid 1800s

MAKING IT PUBLIC

Darwin and Wallace's theories were presented at the Linnean Society, London, in 1858. But their ideas did not get much attention at first. Darwin wrote his theory up as a book, which he titled *On the Origin of Species by Means of Natural Selection* (1859). This book received a lot of interest from the public and the press, which is probably why Darwin's name alone is often linked to evolution. Wallace also wrote a book on evolution, which he called *Darwinism* (1889).

THE EVOLUTION REVOLUTION

So, while the idea of evolution was not new, Darwin and Wallace's theory was revolutionary. This is because they explained how evolution worked by natural selection. Their theory transformed the way people viewed the natural world and humans' place in it. Darwin and Wallace should receive joint credit for their theory, which has since been proved many times over.

NATURAL SELECTION

There are a few different ways that evolution can happen, but one of the main drivers is natural selection. Natural selection has three parts: variation, inheritance and the struggle for existence. The combination of these three things allows groups of individuals from the same species (known as populations) to become adapted to their environments. Eventually, populations can become so different from each other that they form separate species. Darwin and Wallace thought that natural selection worked slowly over millions of years, and mostly it does. However, recent research has shown that sometimes evolution can happen in only a few generations.

VARIATION

Individuals belonging to the same species often have small differences between them, called variations. All living things show variations. For example, the shells of grove snails show variation in colour: they can be pink, yellow or brown, striped or plain. Some of these variations can be found within a single population. Some shell colours are more successful in one area than in another, maybe because they help the snail to camouflage itself.

Grove snails are found across Europe in woodlands, grasslands, parks and gardens.

INHERITANCE

Children (and the young of all living things) inherit variations from their biological parents through reproduction. Variations might be things that you can see, such as a person's height or hair colour. Living things can often resemble one, or both, parents, as well as other relatives. You can see some similarities between the family members in this park. Usually there is quite a bit of variation even within a family.

STRUGGLE FOR EXISTENCE

The struggle for existence controls which variations are successful and which are lost in a population. In the wild, not all living things will survive long enough to have young. The individuals that are most likely to survive and have the most young are those with a variation that makes them better suited to their environment. For example, every oak tree produces thousands of acorns that could grow into new oak trees. However, many acorns and seedlings are eaten. Also, there are not enough resources, such as water and space, for all the acorns to grow into trees. Some species of oak have seedlings with poisonous leaves, which might help to stop them being eaten. These oaks are more likely to thrive and give rise to new trees, which inherit these characteristics.

A DNA PLAYGROUND

Darwin and Wallace came up with their theories of evolution by natural selection before the discovery of deoxyribonucleic acid (DNA). We now know that DNA is a material found in the cells of living things. It works as an instruction manual and controls how an individual grows and develops. Here is how DNA works with variation, inheritance and the struggle for existence.

Variations – These are caused by random changes in DNA, called mutations.

Inheritance – Individuals inherit DNA from their parents, which is how variations are passed onto the next generation.

Struggle for existence – This controls which variations are kept in a population and which are lost.

This climbing frame is shaped like the double helix strands of DNA.

THE GAME OF LIFE

Let's think about natural selection in action in an imaginary meadow. Out in the wild it is a constant battle for survival, and playing the game isn't always easy. Follow the stepping stones and look out for the three main parts of natural selection as you go.

1

It's springtime – the sun is shining, leaves are green and flowers are blooming. One day, some rabbits find the meadow and start eating the delicious plants there.

2

The rabbits munch on the luscious green leaves of the plants. Most of them have smooth leaves but there is **variation** – a few have sharp spines on their leaves, caused by a random mutation in the plant's DNA. The rabbits avoid the spiny-leaved plants because they are painful to eat.

3

The smooth-leaved plants are eaten by the rabbits, who now have lots of young. They all eat so many of the smooth-leaved plants that, after a while, there are hardly any left in the meadow.

4

Each time the smooth-leaved plants grow fresh green shoots, the rabbits eat them! This means most of these plants can't produce flowers and seeds. The **struggle for existence** begins. The spiny-leaved plants have many flowers because the rabbits avoid eating them.

5

In the autumn the spiny-leaved plants produce lots of seeds, which get blown around the meadow. The spiny-leaved characteristic is **inherited** by the next generation of plants.

6 After many years of rabbits living in this meadow, the spiny-leaved plant variation has been very successful. These plants are said to have adapted to their environment. In other words they have been selected by nature – this is known as natural selection.

7 While the smooth-leaved plants may grow elsewhere in a different meadow, they are no longer found here. They have become extinct in this meadow.

8 The smooth-leaved and spiny-leaved plants are now isolated (or separated) from one another and form two populations. After a long time, they may become so different that even if they happen to grow in the same meadow again, they can no longer breed together. They have become two different species.

HAPPILY EVER AFTER... OR IS IT?

Life in the natural world is tough: environments and climates change and species have to adapt to new challenges. But this usually takes a *very* long time. The rabbit and the spiny-leaved plants offer just one imaginary example of evolution, but how else could the animals and plants in the meadow evolve?

Imagine if a crafty fox moved into the meadow and started hunting the rabbits. Fewer rabbits could mean that the smooth-leaved plants have a chance to start growing again from seeds stored in the soil.

Or perhaps a rabbit is born with a mutation that gives it slightly tougher skin around its mouth. This variation would give the rabbit an advantage and allow it to eat the spiny-leaved plants. The spiny-leaved plants would then have less of an advantage in this environment.

Can you think of anything else that could happen in the meadow?

HOW IT ALL BEGAN

HADEAN AND ARCHEAN EONS

Our solar system contains the Sun, eight planets and many moons, comets and space rocks. It was formed after a huge cloud of dust and gas was pulled together by the force of gravity. Some of the debris collected in the centre of the cloud, creating the Sun. The Sun's strong gravity then dragged the rest of the cloud into orbit around it. This formed the Earth and other planets.

1 | *4,600–4,000 MYA* HOT, HOT, HOT

Giant rocks from outer space pummelled Earth. The rocks eventually moulded with the planet and made it bigger. This constant battering also made Earth get hotter, until it became a molten mass of super-hot liquid magma. Heavy, dense substances, like iron and nickel, sank to the centre, forming the metal core. Less dense material rose upwards, becoming the Earth's mantle. Eventually, the surface cooled enough to form solid rock, creating the crust.

2 | *4,200–3,800 MYA* SPLASH!

At the start of its life, Earth was too hot to have liquid water on the surface. But as it cooled down, liquid water appeared. Scientists believe that some of this water came from the original material that created the Earth. They also think water could have been brought here by asteroids and comets that crashed into the planet.

3 | *4,000–2,500 MYA* NURSERIES OF EARLY LIFE

There are many theories about how life appeared on Earth. Some scientists think lightning struck warm ponds that contained just the right chemicals to transform into the building blocks of life. Other scientists think meteorites from space brought life's building blocks to Earth. Still others think the first living things formed around chemical-rich deep ocean vents thousands of metres below the surface of the sea.

THE TIMELINE
MYA means
Million Years Ago

4,600–4,000 MYA
HADEAN
EON

4,000–2,500 MYA
ARCHEAN
EON

2,500–538.8 MYA
PROTEROZOIC
EON

538.8–485.4 MYA
CAMBRIAN
PERIOD

485.4–443.8 MYA
ORDOVICIAN
PERIOD

443.8–419.2 MYA
SILURIAN
PERIOD

419.2–358.9 MYA
DEVONIAN
PERIOD

4 | *3,700–3,500 MYA* THE ORIGINS OF OXYGEN

A type of bacteria called cyanobacteria was one of the first organisms (living things) on Earth, and it still exists today. Cyanobacteria use energy from the Sun and release oxygen as waste. This process is called photosynthesis. Cyanobacteria can live in colonies and create a glue-like substance that sticks rock particles together. This forms underwater reefs called stromatolites.

PIONEERING PEOPLE

Charles Lyell (1797–1875) and **Mary Horner Lyell** (1808–1873) were scientific partners and husband and wife. With the help of Mary, Charles discovered that many natural processes (such as erosion) that could be seen on Earth's surface, had also occurred in the past. Because these natural processes work so slowly, Lyell suggested that the Earth must be much older than previously thought. This discovery allowed Darwin and Wallace to consider that evolution had also taken place very slowly.

5 | *3,300–3,200 MYA* LAND AHOY!

The Earth at this time was a very hostile environment with constant showers of space rocks, such as meteorites and asteroids. The hot ocean bubbled and the atmosphere was mostly made of carbon dioxide and nitrogen gases and water vapour. The first large continents were formed by rock that was pushed up from under the ocean by hot magma that rose up under the crust.

6 | *2,500–2,100 MYA* THE GREAT OXIDATION EVENT

Over time, growing numbers of cyanobacteria released lots of oxygen into the air through their photosynthesis. The high levels of oxygen poisoned the bacteria that were not used to it. Carbon dioxide and methane are greenhouse gases, which keep Earth warm. Lower levels of these gases in the atmosphere led to an ice age, where most of the oceans and land were covered with ice.

PHOTOSYNTHESIS

Photosynthesis is a reaction that happens inside most plants and some bacteria. Photosynthesis is powered by the energy from sunlight. It converts water and carbon dioxide into sugar and oxygen. The sugar provides energy for the organism. Cyanobacteria were most likely the first living things to photosynthesise. Plants did not evolve until much later.

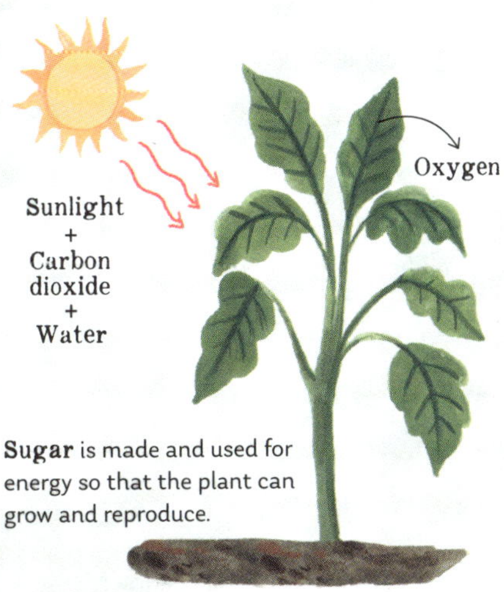

Photosynthesis formula:

Sunlight + Carbon dioxide + Water → Sugar + Oxygen

358.9–298.9 MYA CARBONIFEROUS PERIOD	298.9–251.9 MYA PERMIAN PERIOD	251.9–201.3 MYA TRIASSIC PERIOD	201.3–145 MYA JURASSIC PERIOD	145–66 MYA CRETACEOUS PERIOD	66–23 MYA PALAEOGENE PERIOD	23–2.58 MYA NEOGENE PERIOD	2.58 MYA–Present QUATERNARY PERIOD

PLANET EARTH ROCKS!

Earth has not always looked the way it does now. The land and oceans were once in different places and are still moving even today. Over billions of years, enormous land masses, called supercontinents, formed and then separated. This kind of movement influenced the climate and ocean currents. It also changed the landscape in many ways, such as by forming mountains. All of these changes affected the spread and evolution of living things.

PIONEERING PEOPLE

Alfred Wegener (1880–1930) noticed that some of the continents looked as though they could fit together like puzzle pieces. He studied maps of Earth and different rock types and fossils, and wrote a book called *The Origin of Continents and Oceans*. His book outlined his theory of continental drift, which describes how continents move over time.

THE BIG PUZZLE

Earth is formed in a series of layers, like a cake. The uppermost layer, the lithosphere, is made up of many slabs, called tectonic plates. They float on the Earth's hot, gooey mantle. Tectonic plates can move by anything from a few millimetres to more than five centimetres per year, carrying the continents with them. Large earthquakes and volcanoes can often occur where the plates meet, causing the land to change. These maps show the position of the continents at different moments in Earth's history. We start around 250 million years ago, which was the last time all the continents were joined together in one single land mass.

1.

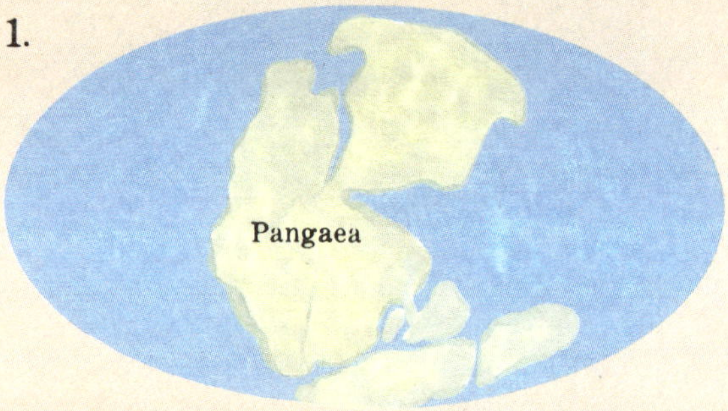

250 million years ago in the Triassic Period (see pages 32–33)
The supercontinent Pangaea was fully formed

2.

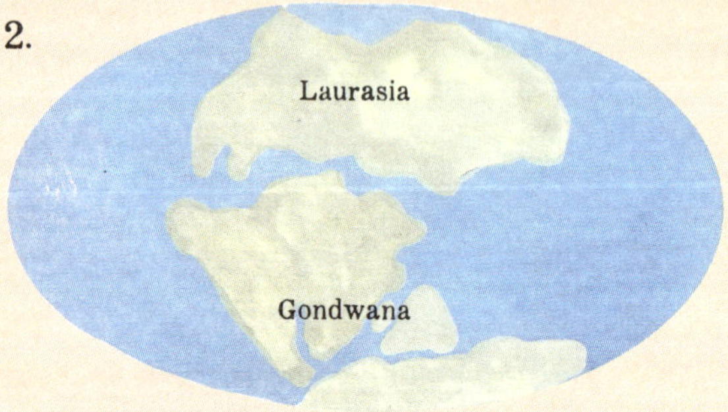

150 million years ago in the Jurassic Period (see pages 32–33)
Pangaea separated into two continents – Laurasia in the north and Gondwana in the south

3.

100 million years ago in the Cretaceous Period (see pages 34–35)
The individual continents gradually moved apart

4.

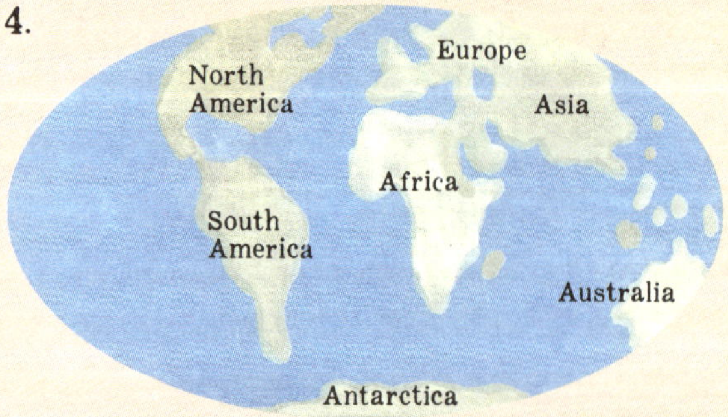

Earth today in the Quaternary Period (see pages 44–49)
The continents are still on the move

5.

The future, around 220 million years from now
It is estimated that a supercontinent will form once more

MOVING RAINFORESTS

As land masses move with the tectonic plates, so do living things. The spread of certain plants and fossils suggests that Australia, Antarctica, South America and New Zealand were once part of Gondwana. There were lots of rainforests on this supercontinent, and many parts of the land were covered with shallow seas. Some of the plants that are found in what is now Australia are relatives of plants that grew in Gondwana.

Queensland's Gondwana Rainforest in modern-day Australia

THE GALÁPAGOS ISLANDS

The Galápagos are a group of islands in the Pacific Ocean about 1,000 kilometres off the coast of Ecuador. The islands sit on the edge of the Nazca tectonic plate and were formed by volcanic activity. When they first formed, the Galápagos Islands were lifeless and the ground was bare, hardened lava. But over time, living things flew, drifted or caught a lift there from distant places. The ocean acted like a barrier and kept the animals and plants on the islands from breeding with those from their original homes or from other islands. This allowed them to evolve independently into new species.

The Galápagos Islands now have many plants, fungi and animals that aren't found anywhere else on Earth. Tortoises, for example, probably floated there from South America and then spread to the different islands, where they have evolved into new species of giant tortoises. When Charles Darwin visited the islands in 1835, he was fascinated to hear that the local people could tell which island a tortoise had come from by the shape of its shell.

Tortoises with a saddle-shaped shell are mainly found on the lower, drier islands. The shape of their shell might allow these tortoises to stretch their necks and reach high-growing plants. Having room to stretch their necks might also help the tortoises right themselves if they end up on their back!

Tortoises with a dome-shaped shell live mainly on islands with moist highland regions where the low-lying plants might be easier to reach.

LIFE FILLS THE SEAS

PROTEROZOIC EON AND CAMBRIAN PERIOD

For billions of years, bacteria and other similar organisms called prokaryotes were the only living things on Earth. But eventually, conditions began to change and more complex organisms started to evolve. The first of these was a group called eukaryotes. They were very important as they led to the evolution of plants, animals and fungi.

1 | *Sometime before 1,800 MYA* FRIENDS FOREVER

Many scientists think eukaryotes were created when one prokaryote swallowed another. The two prokaryotes formed a single organism with one living inside the other. Both prokaryotes benefited from this – the host protected the guest and the guest provided energy. Over time, more living things joined the party. A cyanobacterium was swallowed by a eukaryote and became a chloroplast. The chloroplast could photosynthesise, so it provided the eukaryote with food. These unions enabled eukaryotes to evolve into more complex living things.

A. One prokaryote swallows another. The new prokaryote provides energy and is called a mitochondrion.

B. A new cell, called a eukaryotic cell, is formed. Cells are the basic structures that all living things are made of. This eukaryote evolved into animals and fungi.

C. If the eukaryotic cell swallows a cyanobacterium, the cyanobacterium becomes a chloroplast.

D. The chloroplast can photosynthesise and provide the cell with energy. This eukaryote evolved into plants.

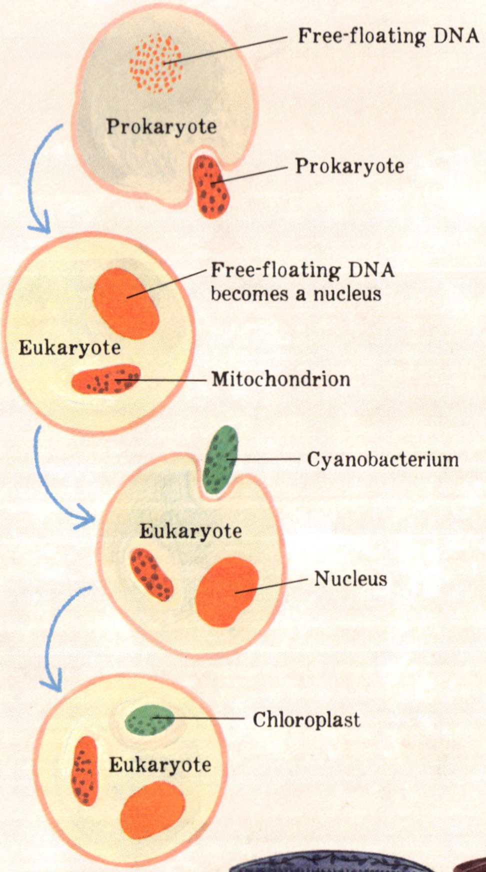

2 | *Around 1,200–1,000 MYA* THE FIRST PLANTS

The first plants were probably similar to seaweeds. Only 2 millimetres long, they grew in the shallow ocean.

PIONEERING PEOPLE

Lynn Margulis (1938–2011) investigated the role of prokaryotic 'hosts and guests' for the evolution of eukaryotes. This completely changed the way that people understood how life began on Earth.

3 | *635–538.8 MYA* THE GARDEN OF EDIACARA

Some of the first animals we know about lived on the ocean floor during a time called the Ediacaran Period, which came at the end of the Proterozoic Eon. Some of them were anchored to the sea floor and others could move freely and graze along it.

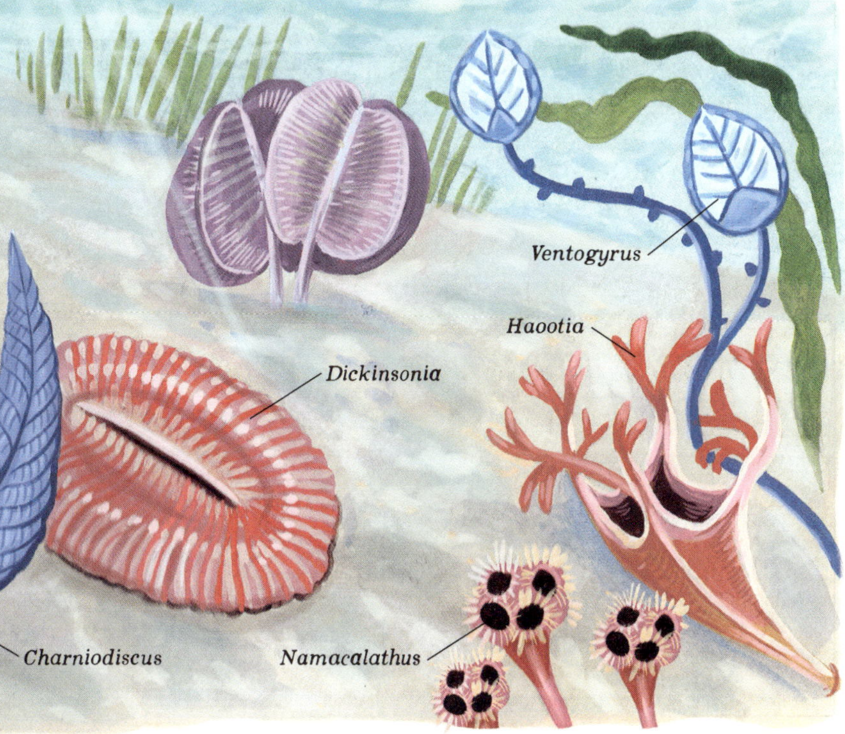

4 | *Around 538.8–485 MYA* NEW SPECIES ON THE BLOCK

Ancestors of some modern animals first appeared during the Cambrian Period in an event called the Cambrian Explosion. Some of these creatures were the first to have hard shells and some were ferocious hunters. At this time, Ediacaran animals became extinct. It's possible that this was because they couldn't compete with these new species, or because there was less oxygen available.

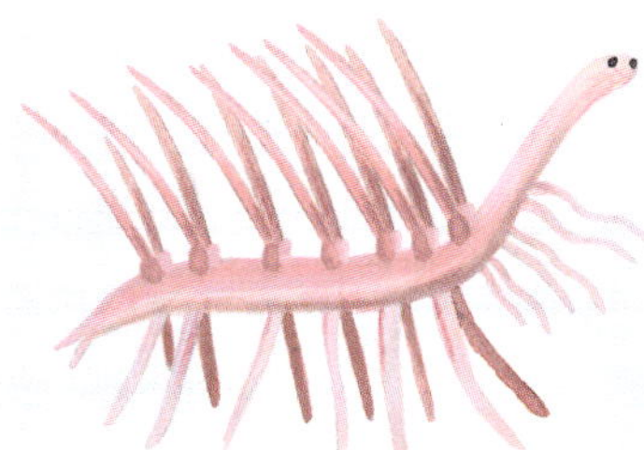

Hallucigenia had long spines on its back, which scientists first mistook for leg-like structures.

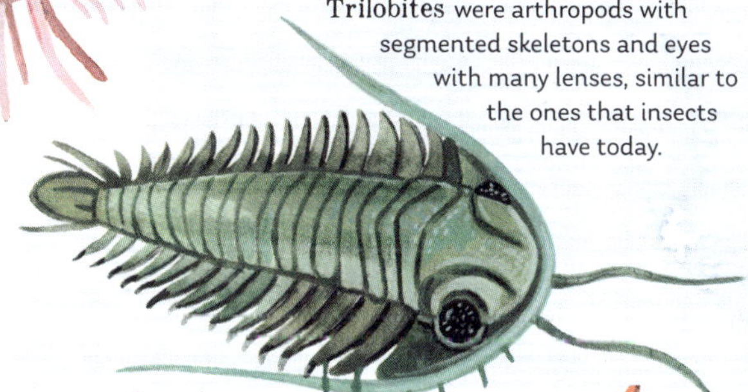

Trilobites were arthropods with segmented skeletons and eyes with many lenses, similar to the ones that insects have today.

Pikaia was a flattened fish-like animal with a fin. It had a notochord, which is similar to the spinal cord found in vertebrates (animals with a backbone).

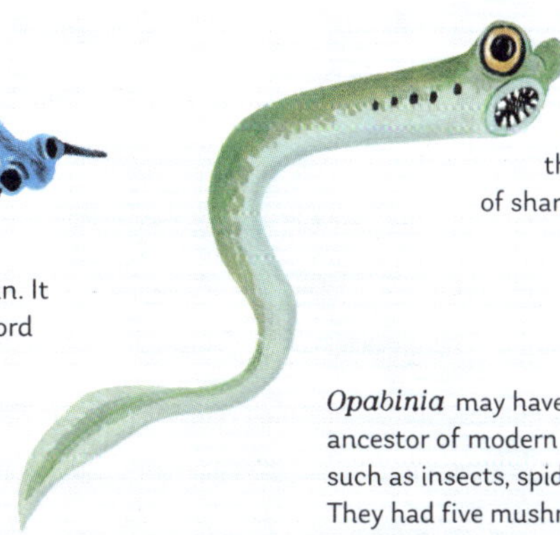

Conodonts were eel-like animals that had many rows of sharp, pointed teeth.

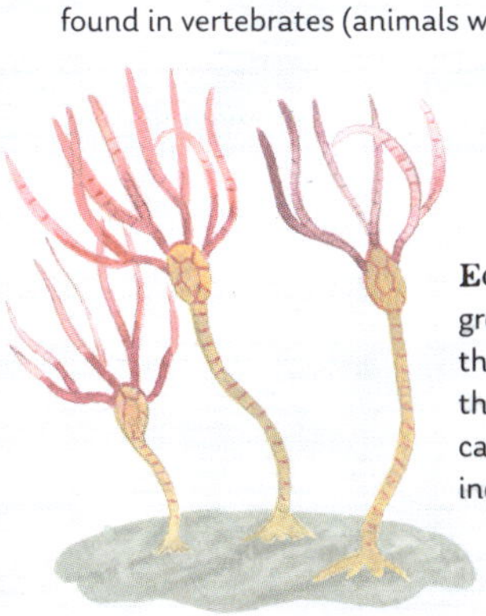

Eocrinoids were animals that grew on the seafloor and filtered the water for food. They were the earliest member of a group called echinoderms, which today includes sea urchins.

Opabinia may have been an ancestor of modern arthropods, such as insects, spiders and crabs. They had five mushroom-shaped eyes and a long nozzle for feeding.

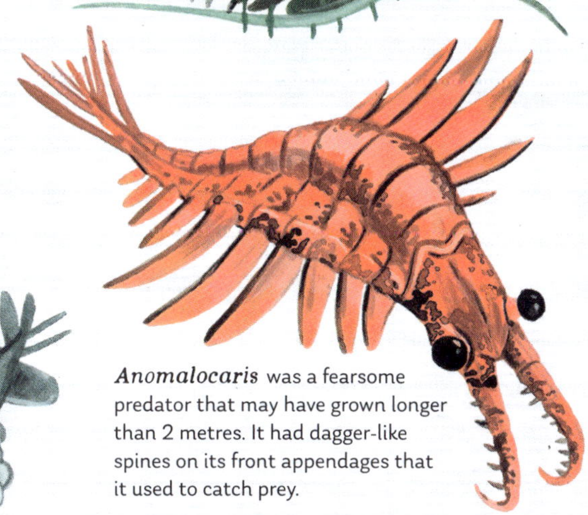

Anomalocaris was a fearsome predator that may have grown longer than 2 metres. It had dagger-like spines on its front appendages that it used to catch prey.

LIFE FINDS A NEW HOME

ORDOVICIAN AND SILURIAN PERIODS

During the Ordovician Period, many parts of the continents were covered in warm, shallow seas that opened up new areas for marine life. Things were also changing on the land, where gigantic tree-like fungi towered over tiny plants that clung to the rocks.

1 | *485.4–443.8 MYA* FIRST LAND PLANTS

Most scientists agree that the first land plants arose during the Ordovician Period. They were small, grew close to the ground and reproduced with spores. Spores are tiny cells that grow into structures from which new plants form. It was possible for land plants to become established thanks to fungi, which digested dead material and helped create soil. Fossil records show that fungi were among the earliest living things on land, possibly appearing up to 1 billion years ago.

Prototaxites was the largest living thing on land during the late Ordovician and Silurian Periods. It is thought to be a fungus and it grew to 8 metres tall!

The millipede-like *Pneumodesmus newmanii* was probably the first animal that crawled on land. It had tiny openings on its body, which allowed it to breathe air.

First land plants

2 | *485.4–443.8 MYA* THE ORDOVICIAN OCEAN

Large reefs, with many kinds of corals, sponges and other animals that lived in colonies, flourished in the ocean. Some of these creatures, such as moss animals (or Bryozoans), are still around today. They live in groups in shell-like structures. Others, such as graptolites, are now extinct.

Graptolites lived in colonies and floated above or sat on the seafloor.

Brachiopods had shells and were attached to the seafloor with a fleshy stalk. They filtered the surrounding water to get their food.

Nautiloids lived in a tube-like protective shell that was up to 5 metres long. They hunted with tentacles, similar to their living relatives, squid and octopuses.

Moss animal (Bryozoan)

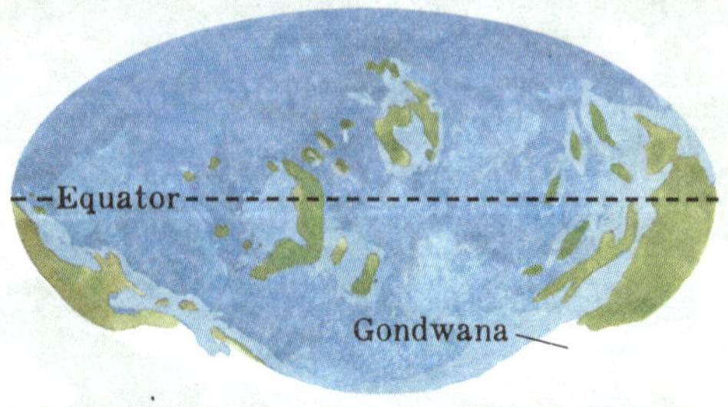

3 | *445.2–443.8 MYA* ORDOVICIAN MASS EXTINCTION

In the late Ordovician, Gondwana moved to the South Pole and became covered by ice. This led to global cooling and a drop in sea levels. Because of this, about 85 per cent of all marine animals became extinct. After this, there was lots of volcanic activity that released carbon dioxide into the air.

THE TIMELINE MYA means Million Years Ago | 4,600–4,000 MYA HADEAN EON | 4,000–2,500 MYA ARCHEAN EON | 2,500–538.8 MYA PROTEROZOIC EON | 538.8–485.4 MYA CAMBRIAN PERIOD | 485.4–443.8 MYA ORDOVICIAN PERIOD | 443.8–419.2 MYA SILURIAN PERIOD | 419.2–358.9 MYA DEVONIAN PERIOD

5 | 433–393 MYA TRANSPORT FOR NUTRIENTS

Cooksonia was the first vascular land plant, which means it had special tubes that carried water and nutrients around inside it. This system also stabilised the plant, even though it was only a few centimetres tall. *Cooksonia* grew close to the water's edge and it reproduced with spores. Scientists believe that root-like structures held it in the soil and took up nutrients and water.

PIONEERING PEOPLE

Shigeru Kuratani (1958–present) studies lampreys and hagfish, which are the only living species of jawless fish. He looks at how their young develop, to see how, and from what part of the head, the jaw might have evolved.

4 | 443.8–419.2 MYA THE SILURIAN OCEAN

After the mass extinction, new life evolved in the ocean. Some of these new creatures were skilful predators.

Sea scorpions called eurypterids were dangerous predators that could grow to over 2.5 metres long. They were armed with claws and spines, which they used to grab and crush prey.

Ammonoids had coiled shells and evolved from the nautiloids.

Ostracoderms, which had first appeared in the Cambrian Period, had an outer skeleton made of tough bony plates and an inner skeleton made of a more flexible tissue called cartilage. These fish were jawless.

THE EVOLUTION OF THE JAW

The evolution of the jawed mouth in fish was very important. It enabled fish to grab and crush their prey, becoming effective predators. Some scientists believe that the jaw in fish evolved from gill arches near the mouth. These arches fused together and transformed into jaw bones.

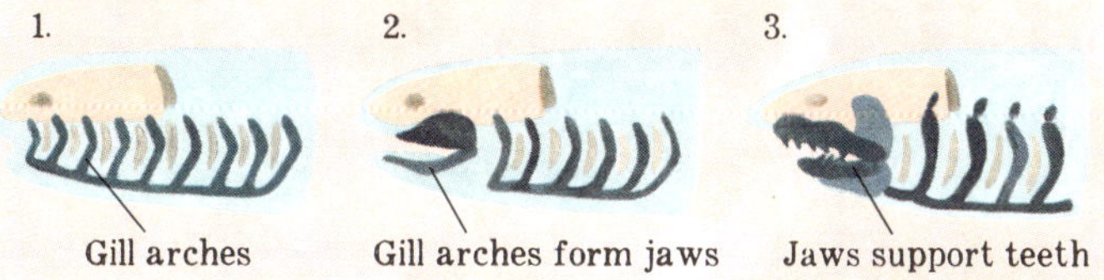

FANTASTIC FOSSILS

Fossils are the preserved remains of once-living things. They are like pieces of a puzzle. Once assembled, they can build a picture of past environments. They can also tell us a lot about the evolution of living things. Fossils typically range from about 10,000 years to well over a billion years old. Without fossils we would know very little about Earth's history.

HOW FOSSILS ARE FORMED

The formation of fossils is a rare event that only happens under special conditions. When living things die, they will usually be eaten by scavengers or decomposed by fungi and bacteria. Occasionally, if the dead thing is buried by sediment, such as volcanic ash or mud, the decay can slow down and its body may turn into a fossil. Different types of fossils form depending on the conditions. Here's how these processes might work with a snail.

① A snail dies.

② The soft parts of its body rot away, leaving only the hard shell behind.

③

IMPRESSION FOSSIL

The shell decays, leaving an impression in the sediment. When this impression is covered by another layer of sediment, the shape of the shell is preserved as a fossil.

Shell impression

↓

Rock with shell impression

***or* CAST**

The snail shell is covered with sediment that hardens to stone. When the shell decays it leaves a hollow mould. The mould is filled by more sediment, which hardens into a rock cast of the shell.

The shell dissolves and the cavity is filled with sediment

↓

Cast of the shell remains

***or* MINERALISATION**

The snail shell is entirely covered with sediment. Minerals seep into the shell from the surroundings, gradually replacing the shell and crystallising. The shell turns into rock.

Shell is replaced with minerals

↓

Shell has turned into rock

LEAVING A TRACE

Animals leave traces behind that can also become fossils. A trace fossil might be a burrow, footprints or even poo (fossilised poo is called coprolite). When animals walk over sludgy mud, they leave footprints. If the mud hardens and the prints get covered by sediment, they might end up as trace fossils.

A giant sloth leaving footprints in the mud

STICKY BUSINESS

Another way that fossils can be formed is when small living things, such as insects, spiders and plant parts, are trapped in sticky tree resin. The resin hardens, and over millions of years, becomes amber.

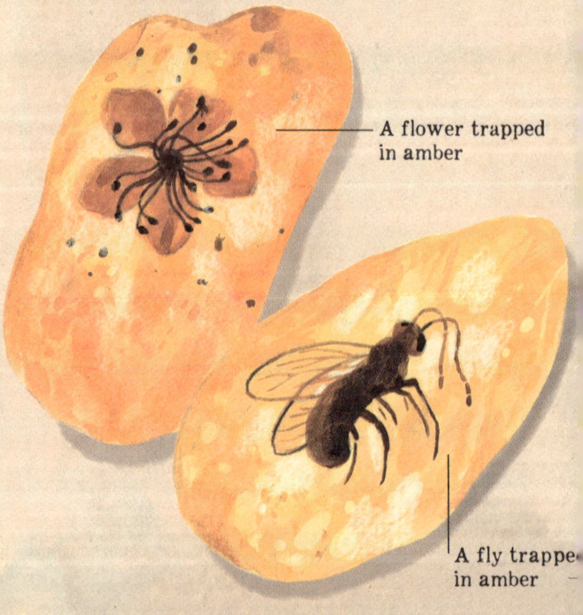

A flower trapped in amber

A fly trappe in amber

MICROFOSSILS

Some fossils, called microfossils, are so tiny that you need a microscope to see them. Microfossils form from living things, such as single-celled algae called diatoms, pollen from flowers and fish scales.

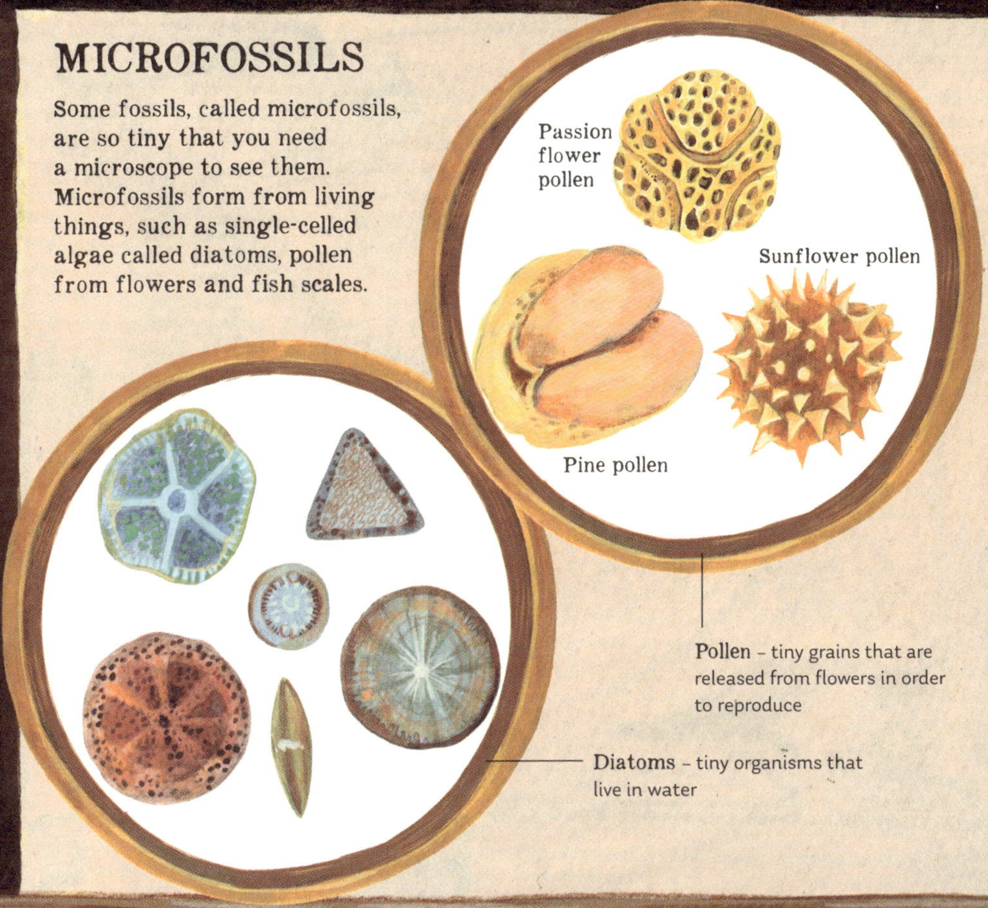

PIONEERING PEOPLE

Mary Anning (1799–1847) collected fossils from the Jurassic Coast in England. Landslides in this area had revealed fossils from the Jurassic Period, which is when dinosaurs were alive. When Mary was 12 years old, she and her older brother found the first fossil ever identified of an extinct marine reptile called an ichthyosaur. Later she also found two plesiosaurs. Mary became a world expert in palaeontology.

HOW TO DATE A FOSSIL

① LOOK FOR LAYERS

One way to figure out the age of a fossil is by seeing how deep it is buried. Older fossils are usually found in the lower layers of rock, while the younger ones are nearer the top.

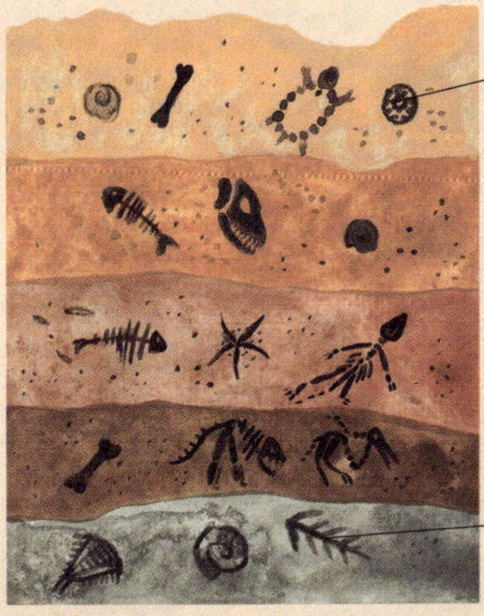

② SEARCH FOR NEIGHBOURS

If we know how old certain fossils are, we can work out the age of any others that are found nearby. For example, *Parapuzosia seppenradensis*, the largest ammonite in the world, lived about 80 million years ago. Any fossils found near to it would likely be around the same age.

Parapuzosia seppenradensis fossil

③ EXAMINE THE ELEMENTS

Radioactive elements naturally occur in a type of rock called igneous rock. These elements change into new elements over time, and we know how long this takes to happen. Scientists can compare the amount of the original element in the rock (shown here as the yellow dots) to the amount of the new element (the blue dots) to figure out the age of the rock. By calculating the age of the rock above and below the fossil, scientists can work out an age range for the fossil.

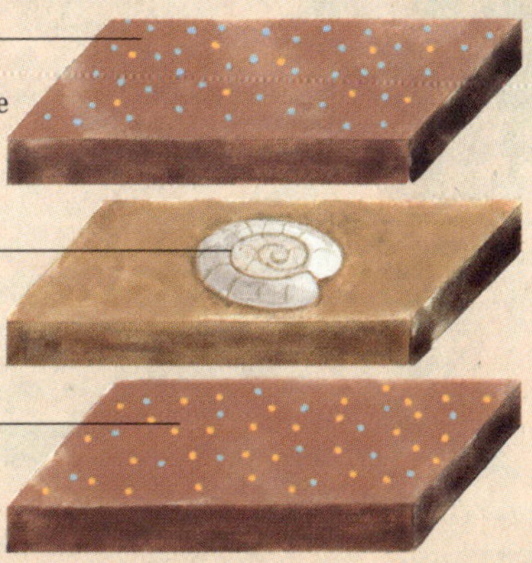

ANIMALS FIND THEIR FEET

DEVONIAN PERIOD

The Devonian Period was a time of many new beginnings. New fish groups emerged, later giving rise to vertebrate animals that could live on land. The first woody plants with leaves and seeds evolved, becoming a new source of food and habitats for animals. At the end of this period, all major groups of land plants – except for flowering plants – had evolved.

1 | *419.2–290 MYA* SPINY SHARKS

By the Devonian, spiny sharks (acanthodians) were found in the oceans in large numbers. They had slender bodies and large eyes, spiny fins for defence and scaly bodies for protection. They were probably the ancestors of modern sharks.

Ray-finned fish

2 | *Over 400 MYA* EVOLUTION OF BONY FISH

Fish with bony skeletons evolved towards the end of the Silurian Period. In the Devonian Period, they split into two main groups: ray-finned fish and lobe-finned fish. The ray-finned fish are the largest group of fish still alive today and include goldfish and salmon.

3 | *382–358 MYA* PLACODERM GIANTS

Placoderms were jawed, armoured fish that first arose in the Silurian Period, but really thrived in the Devonian Period. One of the largest was *Dunkleosteus*, which grew to 7 metres long. It was a fierce predator and had bony plates in its mouth that it used for chewing.

4 | *410 MYA and onwards* SWAMP DWELLERS

Early land plants grew in and around swamps. They developed relationships with types of fungi called mycorrhizae that lived underground. The mycorrhizae were connected to the root-like structures of the plants and provided them with nutrients. The fungi got the nutrients from matter that they broke down in the soil. In return, the plants produced and shared sugar. Many small animals also lived in this environment, both in water and on land.

THE TIMELINE MYA means Million Years Ago	4,600–4,000 MYA HADEAN EON	4,000–2,500 MYA ARCHEAN EON	2,500–538.8 MYA PROTEROZOIC EON	538.8–485.4 MYA CAMBRIAN PERIOD	485.4–443.8 MYA ORDOVICIAN PERIOD	443.8–419.2 MYA SILURIAN PERIOD	419.2–358.9 MYA DEVONIAN PERIOD

5 | *Around 390 MYA* THE FIRST TREE TRUNKS

The first plant with wood and leaves was *Archaeopteris*, a tree that formed one of Earth's first forests. Wood helps plants support themselves and enables them to grow larger. Another important evolutionary development was the leaf. Leaves increase the surface area of the plant to maximise photosynthesis.

7 | *385 MYA* FROM SPORES TO SEED

The first plant with seeds evolved. This allowed plants to live away from water. Seeds protect the embryo (the part of the seed that develops into the plant) from drying out. Seeds also have an inner layer that serves as food for the developing plant.

8 | *371–359 MYA* MASS EXTINCTION, AGAIN!

There are several theories about what caused the mass extinction at the end of the Devonian Period. Some scientists believe that the new plants released nutrients from the land into the oceans. This caused the amount of oxygen in the water to drop. The plants also used up lots of the carbon dioxide in the air, making the planet cool, glaciers grow and sea levels drop. About three quarters of the creatures in the seas went extinct.

Elpistostege had gills and lungs, so it could breathe both in and out of water.

6 | *390–365 MYA* FROM FINS TO LIMBS

Lobe-finned fish are thought to be the ancestors of all land vertebrates (animals with backbones). They had special bones that connected their front fins to their shoulders and back fins to their pelvis. These bones later evolved into limbs. *Elpistostege* was a lobe-finned fish that had muscular fins, which allowed it to push itself onto dry land.

PIONEERING PEOPLE

Emilia Ivanovna Vorobyeva (1934–2016) studied fossil fish as well as living vertebrates. She investigated the connection between land vertebrate limbs and lobe-finned fish.

GIANTS FROM THE SWAMPS

CARBONIFEROUS PERIOD

During this time, wet and warm swamps formed around the equator. They were habitats for gigantic flying insects and the first vertebrate animals that lived entirely outside of water.

Horsetail trees (*Calamites*)

1 | *358–305 MYA* SWAMPS FORMED THE CARBONIFEROUS COAL

The dominant swamp plants were tree-sized club mosses and ferns. Once the plants died, they were quickly buried, which slowed their decay. Eventually they turned into coal. Since the 18th century, coal has been mined and burned to create electricity and heat homes.

Seed fern (*Medullosa*)

Tree fern (*Psaronius*)

Delitzschala is thought by many scientists to be the oldest known winged insect. It had a wingspan of around 2.5 centimetres.

2 | *Around 348 MYA* STEP-BY-STEP

The movement of some vertebrate animals from water to land was a gradual process. But, by the early Carboniferous Period, the first fully land-living vertebrates had evolved. These animals had strong limbs and backbones that could support their bodies out of water. They also had eyes on top of their heads, which helped improve their vision on land.

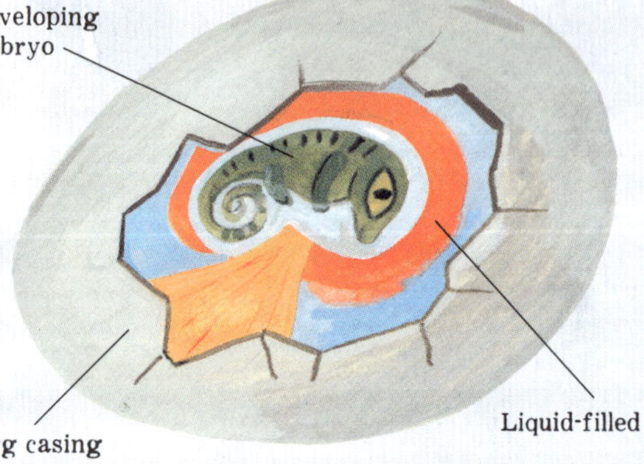

3 | *340 MYA* A PRIVATE POND

Land vertebrates evolved an exciting evolutionary step – the amniotic egg. This egg had a casing with a liquid-filled sac inside that allowed the developing young to float. The evolution of the amniotic egg freed vertebrates from the water and allowed them to take advantage of habitats on land.

Meganeura was the largest dragonfly and had a wingspan of 70 centimetres.

4 | *325 MYA* TAKING TO THE SKIES

Insects existed by the Devonian Period, but during the Carboniferous they formed many new species and spread far and wide. Insects were the first animals to develop the ability to fly.

Club mosses (*Lepidodendron*)

5 | *Around 323.2–298.9 MYA* GIANT INSECTS AND OTHER ARTHROPODS

During this period, some arthropods (creatures with an exoskeleton and jointed limbs, such as insects, lobsters and spiders) grew to enormous sizes. There are several theories as to why this happened. We know that there were higher levels of oxygen in the atmosphere, likely caused by the photosynthesis of the swamp plants. So one theory is that this oversupply of oxygen allowed insects and other arthropods to evolve larger bodies. Another theory is that there were no flying predators to spot and eat the insects and arthropods that grew larger.

PIONEERING PEOPLE

Alfred Sherwood Romer (1894–1973) studied land-dwelling vertebrates, such as ancient amphibians and reptiles, and how they were related to each other.

6 | *305 MYA* THE COAL SWAMPS COLLAPSE

Over a long time, dead swamp plants gathered and were fossilised as coal. They naturally stored carbon dioxide, preventing it from being released into the atmosphere. Less carbon dioxide in the atmosphere led to global cooling (again!). Glaciers spread and almost reached the equator. With more water locked up as ice, the sea level dropped. At the same time, the continents moved closer together, the climate became drier and the lush swamps gradually shrank. Many plants died out, including the giant, tree-like horsetails such as *Calamites*.

Some scorpions such as *Pulmonoscorpius* grew up to 70 centimetres long.

Eryops was a 2-metre long monster that first appeared in the late Carboniferous but become dominant during the later Permian Period. It was a fierce meat eater that swallowed its prey whole.

7 | *300 MYA* MIGHTY PREDATORS

Amphibians were among the first vertebrates that lived most of their lives on land. Most modern amphibians are small animals, such as frogs and toads, but they were once enormous. Like frogs today, they laid their eggs in water and their young had gills, like tadpoles. The young transformed into adults with lungs, allowing them to live on land.

Millipedes such as *Arthropleura* grew to 2.4 metres long.

358.9–298.9 MYA CARBONIFEROUS PERIOD

298.9–251.9 MYA PERMIAN PERIOD

251.9–201.3 MYA TRIASSIC PERIOD

201.3–145 MYA JURASSIC PERIOD

145–66 MYA CRETACEOUS PERIOD

66–23 MYA PALAEOGENE PERIOD

23–2.58 MYA NEOGENE PERIOD

2.58 MYA–Present QUATERNARY PERIOD

FROM ICEHOUSE TO HOTHOUSE

PERMIAN PERIOD

By the start of the Permian Period, large land masses had come together to form the supercontinent Pangaea. Because Pangaea was so big, moisture from the sea could not reach its centre. This caused the climate to heat up, deserts to form and glaciers and ice caps to melt. The land vertebrates that could cope with these hot, dry conditions became dominant. The Permian ended with the most severe mass extinction that Earth has ever known.

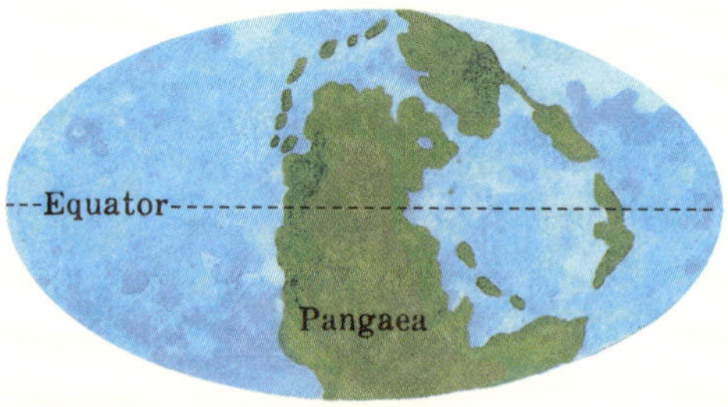

1 | *298.9 MYA and onwards* REPTILES ADAPT

During this time, the land was crawling with many species of reptiles. They were well adapted to the dry climate because their scaly skin stopped their bodies from losing water. Most reptiles were, and still are, cold-blooded. This means they can't maintain their body temperature and have to sunbathe to get warm. Early reptiles were small but gradually evolved to have larger bodies.

Coelurosauravus had wing-like flaps of skin that it used to glide from tree to tree.

Scutosaurus had tough plates for protection.

Eudibamus was only 25 centimetres long and was one of the first animals to move on two legs.

2 | *298.9 MYA and onwards* SYNAPSIDS THRIVE

A new group of animals, called synapsids, had evolved in the Carboniferous Period. During the Permian, they branched off into many new species.

Diictodon dug burrows, in which to sleep and care for its young.

Dimetrodon was a carnivore with a large sail on its back. Scientists think *Dimetrodon* used its sail to help control its body temperature. It may also have been used to attract mates or scare off other animals.

Moschops had a thick skull, which might have been useful for head-butting rivals.

THE TIMELINE MYA means Million Years Ago	4,600–4,000 MYA HADEAN EON	4,000–2,500 MYA ARCHEAN EON	2,500–538.8 MYA PROTEROZOIC EON	538.8–485.4 MYA CAMBRIAN PERIOD	485.4–443.8 MYA ORDOVICIAN PERIOD	443.8–419.2 MYA SILURIAN PERIOD	419.2–358.9 MYA DEVONIAN PERIOD

PIONEERING PEOPLE

Birbal Sahni (1891–1949) was a palaeobotanist – someone who examines fossilised plants. One of the plants that he studied (called *Glossopteris*) helped show that India was once part of the supercontinent Pangaea. The plant was found in parts of the world that were were once together but are no longer connected.

3 | *Around 290 MYA onwards* PROTECTIVE CONES

Seed plants called gymnosperms first arose in the Devonian Period but became dominant during the Permian. The seeds of gymnosperms aren't enclosed by fruits, instead they are protected by cones. Gymnosperms' leaves have a thick waxy coating, which reduces water loss and allows them to grow in dry areas.

Cycads still grow in many parts of the world. The seeds inside their cones can be brightly coloured.

Voltziales were ancestors of living conifers, such as pine trees.

Ginkgophytes are represented by one species today, the maidenhair tree (*Ginkgo bilboa*). Their fleshy seeds often resemble fruits.

4 | *Around 270 MYA and onwards* BECOMING A MAMMAL

Some synapsids gradually evolved unique mammal-like features, such as having fur, and later evolved into mammals. Synapsid fossils from the Permian provide some evidence of this early evolution.

Procynosuchus was a synapsid and an ancestor of mammals. It used its powerful tail to swim in a similar way to a modern crocodile.

JAWSOME HEARING

Mammals have good hearing, in part due to three small inner ear bones called ossicles. These tiny bones – known as the incus, stapes and malleus – evolved from jaw bones. This transition from jaw to ossicles can be seen in synapsid fossils. So mammals, including humans, actually hear with their ancient jaw!

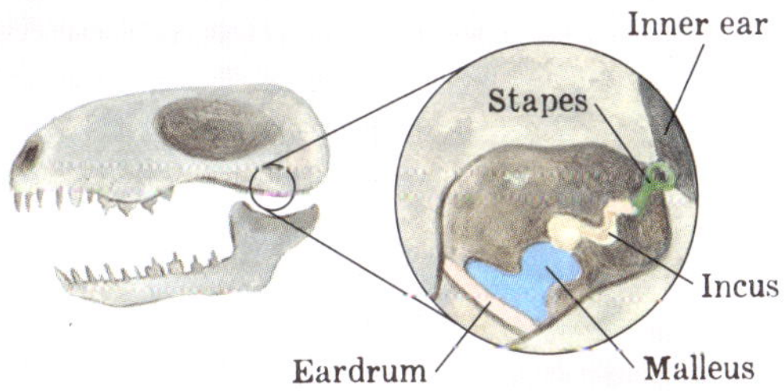

5 | *Around 252 MYA* END-PERMIAN MASS EXTINCTION

Massive volcanic eruptions spewed climate-wrecking gases into the atmosphere for more than one million years. This caused global warming and the extinction of most land species and nearly all sea life.

358.9–298.9 MYA CARBONIFEROUS PERIOD

298.9–251.9 MYA PERMIAN PERIOD

251.9–201.3 MYA TRIASSIC PERIOD

201.3–145 MYA JURASSIC PERIOD

145–66 MYA CRETACEOUS PERIOD

66–23 MYA PALAEOGENE PERIOD

23–2.58 MYA NEOGENE PERIOD

2.58 MYA–Present QUATERNARY PERIOD

THE CAUSES OF CLIMATE CHANGE

'Climate' describes overall weather conditions and patterns, such as temperature and rainfall, over a long period of time. That's not to be confused with weather, which refers to a particular event, for example a sunny day or a storm. Earth's climate has changed gradually throughout history, caused by several different factors. About 200 years ago, humans became one of those factors.

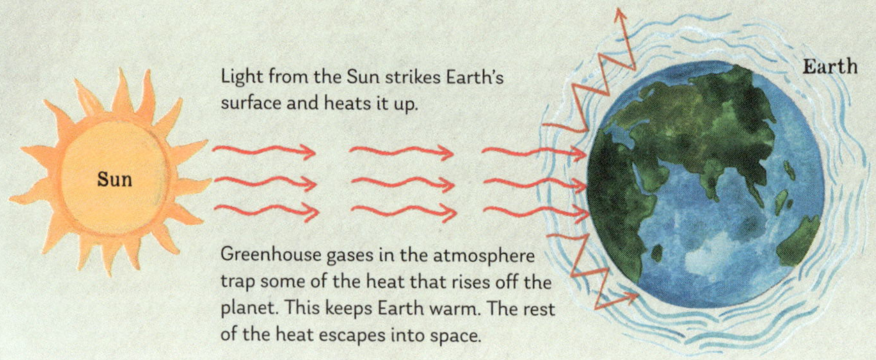

HOW TO GET WARM

Earth is the right temperature for life because certain gases in the atmosphere hold in heat, just like the glass in a greenhouse does. During Earth's history, these greenhouse gases, such as carbon dioxide and methane, were released into the air by volcanic eruptions and other natural processes. When the amount of greenhouse gas went down, Earth cooled. When the amount went up, Earth got hotter.

THE MILANKOVITCH CYCLES

For the past 2.5 million years, Earth has been switching between cold and warm periods. Scientists think that regular changes in Earth's orbit and the way it spins result in periodic increases and decreases in how much energy gets to us from the Sun. These warming and cooling cycles are called Milankovitch cycles.

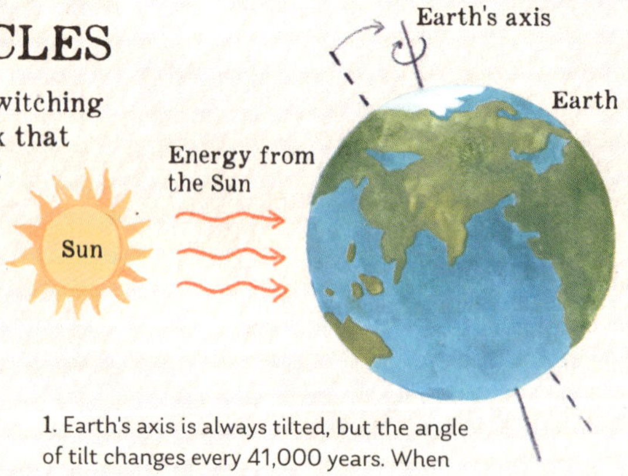

1. Earth's axis is always tilted, but the angle of tilt changes every 41,000 years. When the angle is larger, Earth's polar regions lean towards the Sun. They receive more direct sunlight and heat up more in summer. When the angle is smaller, Earth's poles lean away, receiving less direct sunlight so they don't heat up as much.

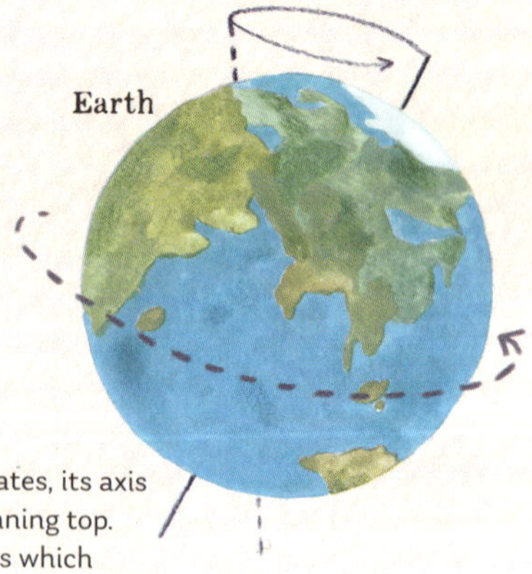

2. When Earth rotates, its axis wobbles like a spinning top. This wobble affects which parts of Earth are tilted towards the Sun at different times of the year.

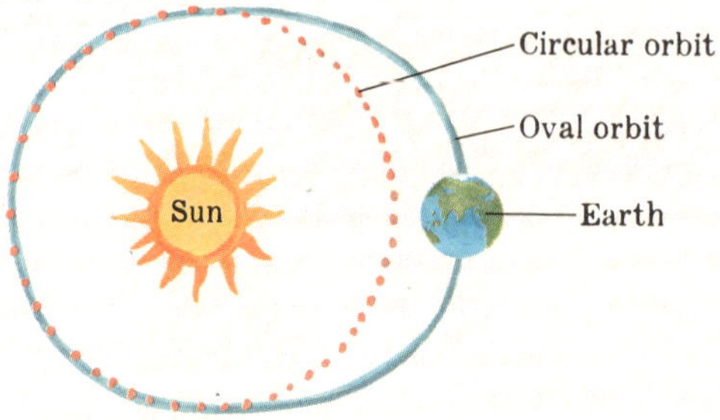

3. Earth's orbit – the path that it takes around the Sun – has an effect, too. The shape of Earth's orbit is almost a circle, but over periods of 100,000 years it gets slightly more stretched out. When this happens, Earth travels both closer to and further from the Sun over the course of a year.

PIONEERING PEOPLE

The Milankovitch cycles were named after **Milutin Milankovitch** (1879–1958). He calculated how Earth's orbit and the tilt of its axis changed the incoming energy from the Sun. Milutin's ideas helped explain some causes of natural climate change. His calculations are still used today.

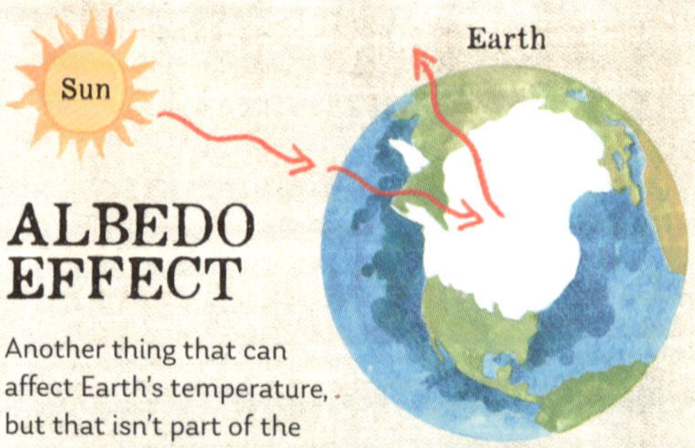

ALBEDO EFFECT

Another thing that can affect Earth's temperature, but that isn't part of the Milankovitch cycles, is called the Albedo Effect. This happens when large areas of the Earth are covered with ice. Pale surfaces like ice or snow reflect more solar energy than dark, bare soil. So, when there is more ice, the planet cools down.

EXTINCTION OF MEGAFAUNA

Earth's changing climate can have a big impact on the biodiversity of an area. Some scientists believe that a change in climate around 10,000–20,000 years ago caused the giant animals that roamed North America to go extinct. Many scientists also think that humans contributed to this extinction by hunting the animals.

THE CURRENT CLIMATE CRISIS

Greenhouse gases occur naturally in the atmosphere. However, over the last 200 years the level of many of them has greatly increased. This is largely due to human activities, such as burning fossil fuels for power and farming animals. Burning fossil fuels releases carbon dioxide, and farming animals, such as cows, causes methane to be released into the atmosphere (from their burps and farts). As the amount of these and other greenhouse gases rises, more heat is trapped on Earth's surface, causing the current climate crisis.

DINOSAURS IN CHARGE

TRIASSIC AND JURASSIC PERIODS

After the Permian mass extinction, many new living things evolved. While some reptiles invaded the sea, dinosaurs large and small started to conquer the land. Shifting tectonic plates caused Pangaea to split in two and large oceans began to form between the land masses. This led to more rainfall as water evaporated along the newly formed coastlines.

Eoraptor

2 | *225–190 MYA* ONE OF THE FIRST DINOSAURS

Eoraptor was a 1-metre-long dinosaur with light, hollow bones. *Eoraptor* had two sets of teeth and may have preyed on insects and small reptiles, but also ate plants.

Nothosaurus

1 | *251–145.5 MYA* THE BIGGEST REPTILES OF THE SEA

Nothosaurs (251–210 MYA) were swimming reptiles that hunted fish to eat. They could also crawl onto land to warm up in the sun and lay eggs. Ichthyosaurs (251–90 MYA) however, spent all their lives in the water. They looked a little like dolphins and most were about 3 metres long. One species called *Shastasaurus pacificus* grew to over 20 metres long – almost twice as long as a bus.

Ichthyosaurus

WHAT IS A DINOSAUR?

Dinosaurs were a group of reptiles, but had certain features that set them apart. Unlike most reptiles' legs, which are sprawled out to the sides, dinosaurs' legs were directly beneath their bodies, giving them an upright stance. These straight legs could support a heavier body and allow for swift movement. Dinosaurs lived on land and laid eggs. Some also had small, coloured feathers.

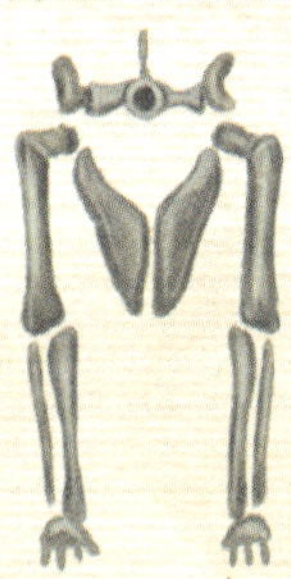

Dinosaurs' legs

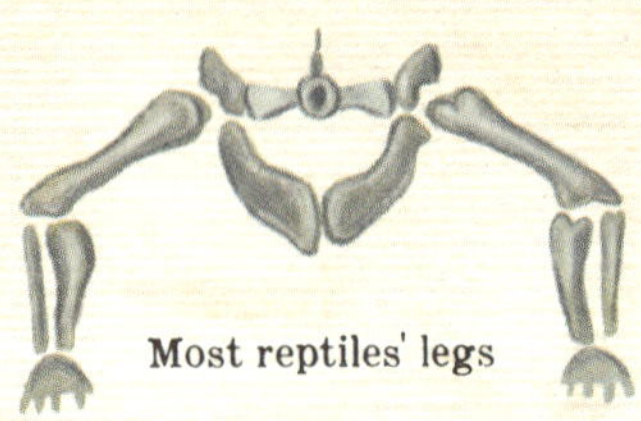

Most reptiles' legs

3 | *Around 201 MYA* END-TRIASSIC MASS EXTINCTION

At the end of the Triassic Period, massive volcanic eruptions released large amounts of greenhouse and other gases. This caused sudden global warming and made the oceans more acidic. Almost three quarters of all the species on Earth went extinct. It is not known why, but dinosaurs survived and went on to become the dominant land animals of the Jurassic and Cretaceous Periods.

THE TIMELINE MYA means Million Years Ago

4,600–4,000 MYA HADEAN EON

4,000–2,500 MYA ARCHEAN EON

2,500–538.8 MYA PROTEROZOIC EON

538.8–485.4 MYA CAMBRIAN PERIOD

485.4–443.8 MYA ORDOVICIAN PERIOD

443.8–419.2 MYA SILURIAN PERIOD

419.2–358.9 MYA DEVONIAN PERIOD

PIONEERING PEOPLE

Anusuya Chinsamy-Turan (1962–present) studies dinosaur bones under the microscope. She found out that dinosaur bones show growth rings (just like trees do). By counting the rings, she came up with a system to estimate the ages of individual dinosaurs.

Cypress tree

Giraffatitan was about 13 metres tall.

4 | *201–65 MYA* ENORMOUS VEGETARIANS

Sauropods were the tallest dinosaurs that we know of. Plant eaters, such as *Giraffatitan* and *Diplodocus*, had extremely long necks for reaching leaves high in the treetops. Their constant munching changed the landscapes by creating open forests.

Monkey puzzle tree

Diplodocus grew up to 30 metres long.

6 | *Around 168–145 MYA* TOUGH PLATES

Stegosaurus was a herbivore that had bony plates along its back. The plates could have made the dinosaur appear larger and help it scare off predators. Or perhaps their plates helped regulate the dinosaur's body temperature by warming its blood in the sunlight or releasing heat to cool down.

Stegosaurus

Cycad tree

Ginkgo tree

5 | *Around 200 MYA* MINIATURE MAMMALS

Early mammals were very small. *Morganucodon*, for example, only grew up to 10 centimetres long. When *Morganucodon* closed its jaw, its back teeth interlocked. This feature is shared by all mammals and allows them to chew their prey. Most reptiles are unable to chew their food and either just swallow it whole or tear off chunks to gulp down.

Morganucodon

358.9–298.9 MYA CARBONIFEROUS PERIOD

298.9–251.9 MYA PERMIAN PERIOD

251.9–201.3 MYA TRIASSIC PERIOD

201.3–145 MYA JURASSIC PERIOD

145–66 MYA CRETACEOUS PERIOD

66–23 MYA PALAEOGENE PERIOD

23–2.58 MYA NEOGENE PERIOD

2.58 MYA–Present QUATERNARY PERIOD

T. REX AND THE RISE OF FLOWERS

CRETACEOUS PERIOD

During this period the climate was very warm, even towards the North and South Poles. Dinosaurs dominated life on land and a new group of plants – the flowering plants – became more varied, transforming life on Earth.

1 | *Around 145–66 MYA* NEW PREDATORS AND PREY

Lots of new species of dinosaurs evolved at this time, and towards the end of the period the land was teeming with them. One of the most fearsome was *Tyrannosaurus rex*. *T. rex* had 60 sharp teeth in its jaw and a super-strength bite. It would have preyed on other dinosaurs, such as *Triceratops*, which had three horns on its head to defend itself, and the duck-billed *Parasaurolophus*.

2 | *145–66 MYA* GIANT REPTILES OF THE SKY

Pterosaurs were flying reptiles that first appeared in the Late Triassic. Some were small, but others were enormous, with wingspans of up to 12 metres. They were the first creatures after insects who evolved to flap their wings and fly.

3 | *145–66 MYA* GIANT REPTILES OF THE OCEANS

The top ocean carnivores were mosasaurs (101–66 MYA) and plesiosaurs (203–66 MYA). Some of these reptiles could grow up to 15 metres long. They hunted other marine reptiles, fish, shellfish and possibly even pterosaurs!

4 | *Around 140 MYA and onwards*
THE RISE OF FLOWERING PLANTS

Many scientists believe that flowering plants (called angiosperms) probably appeared before the Cretaceous Period, but during this time their numbers dramatically increased. These plants had many features that made them successful, such as large leaves, flowers and fruit.

Flowers
Before flowers evolved, a plant's pollen was usually carried and dispersed by the wind. Once flowers evolved, insects became part of the process, transporting pollen while collecting the nectar and pollen that they ate as food.

Fruit
Flowering plants spread with the help of fruits that contained their seeds. Animals will often eat the fruit and the seeds are transported in their guts. The seeds are then released in the animals' droppings and the plants grow in new locations.

Leaves
Flowering plants often have large leaves with many veins. This structure helps with photosynthesis and allows better transport of water and nutrients around the plant. As a result, flowering plants can grow quickly.

5 | *125–80 MYA*
FLOWER POWER

Flowering plants had a massive impact on Earth. They created food and new habitats for other living things. Their large, fast-growing leaves released water vapour into the atmosphere. This created more clouds and rainfall and impacted climates, particularly in the tropics.

6 | *66–65 MYA*
ASTEROID, DEAD AHEAD!

A huge asteroid collided with Earth. This is thought to have caused around 75 per cent of all living things, including all dinosaurs (except birds), to become extinct. The impact threw giant dust clouds into the atmosphere, partially blocking out the sun. The dust caused temperatures to drop, killing many plants. Fewer plants meant plant eaters died, and fewer plant eaters meant meat eaters died. Following the impact the oceans turned acidic, killing off many marine species, too.

PIONEERING PEOPLE

Luis Alvarez (1911–1988), his son **Walter Alvarez** (1940–present), **Frank Asaro** (1927–2014) and **Helen V. Michel** (1932–present) studied rock samples of the Late Cretaceous mass extinction. They found high concentrations of the element iridium, which is common in asteroids but very rare on Earth. This provided evidence that the Cretaceous mass extinction was caused by an asteroid impact.

358.9–298.9 MYA CARBONIFEROUS PERIOD | 298.9–251.9 MYA PERMIAN PERIOD | 251.9–201.3 MYA TRIASSIC PERIOD | 201.3–145 MYA JURASSIC PERIOD | 145–66 MYA CRETACEOUS PERIOD | 66–23 MYA PALAEOGENE PERIOD | 23–2.58 MYA NEOGENE PERIOD | 2.58 MYA–Present QUATERNARY PERIOD

EVOLVING TOGETHER

All species of living things interact with other species out in the wild. This can cause them to evolve together in a process called coevolution. Flowers and their pollinators offer some great examples of coevolution, and sometimes become completely dependent on one another. These species are then linked together in the never-ending dance of evolution.

POLLINATION PALS

Pollinators are animals, such as some insects, birds, bats or other small mammals, that carry pollen between flowers. These animals feed on the flower's sweet nectar or pollen. When a pollinator visits a flower, some pollen grains can get stuck to its body. As the animal travels between flowers, the pollen can brush off in the next flower. The pollen fertilises the plant, allowing it to make seeds. Some pollinators are attracted to flowers because of their colour or scent, or even because they look like a potential mate!

THE ORCHID AND THE MOTH

In 1862, Charles Darwin was sent a curious flower to study – an orchid from Madagascar. Darwin looked at the flower and noticed that it kept its nectar at the bottom of a 30-centimetre-long tube. He predicted that its pollinator must have an equally long tongue to reach the nectar. A few years later, Wallace predicted this orchid's pollinator would be a type of hawk moth. Eventually, Darwin and Wallace were both proved right, and we now know that this orchid and moth must have coevolved over time.

HOW IT WORKS

Coevolution takes place gradually by natural selection. In the case of this orchid and moth, they both probably had ancestors with slight variations, such as tubes and tongues of different lengths. Over time, the flowers with the long tubes and the moths with the long tongues became most successful. The moth had to compete with other species for the orchid's nectar, but its long tongue meant that it was better suited to the long-tubed flower. Perhaps the other competitors died out or found other food sources. It is helpful for the moth to have its own source of nectar and for the orchid to have a reliable pollinator. It's a win-win situation!

When the hawk moth isn't slurping up nectar, it keeps its 30-centimetre tongue rolled up out of the way.

COEVOLUTION COMBAT

Sometimes coevolution benefits both species, but other times two (or more) species are working against one another. Take the milkweed plant and the caterpillar of the monarch butterfly, for example. The caterpillar likes to munch on the milkweed's leaves, so the plant evolved dense hairs to protect itself. But the caterpillar then evolved to nibble the hair off before eating the leaf! So the milkweed evolved a way to make a poisonous liquid. But the caterpillar evolved so that it could tolerate the poison. Each time the plant finds a new way to protect itself, the caterpillar finds a way around the obstacle. Both species coevolve: one to protect itself and the other to feed itself safely.

PIONEERING PEOPLE

Anurag Agrawal (1972–present) is an expert in coevolution in milkweed plants and monarch butterflies. He recently found out that monarch caterpillars are able to convert the milkweed's poison into less harmful substances.

THE AGE OF MAMMALS

PALAEOGENE PERIOD

The first mammals evolved in the Triassic Period and were small. In the Palaeogene Period, with the dinosaurs extinct, thousands of new species evolved. Land bridges allowed many living things to move between continents. With the exception of a few hot spells, the climate was becoming cooler and drier.

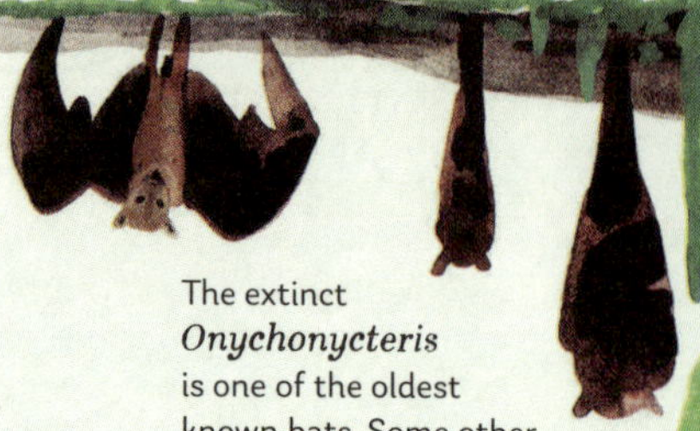

The extinct *Onychonycteris* is one of the oldest known bats. Some other mammals can glide, but bats are the only ones that can flap their wings to fly.

Eomys was a small animal that is thought to be related to gophers. But unlike its modern relatives, it could glide through the air.

1 | *Around 66–41 MYA* FORESTS FLOURISHED

Many new species of flowering plants evolved, including some that can still be found today. The warm spells allowed forests to spread across the globe, even to the ice-free poles. Tropical plants and mangrove forests even grew in Europe.

Paraceratherium is believed to have been the biggest land mammal of all time. This relative of the rhino measured 5 metres to the shoulder.

Some forests at this time contained a mixture of tropical plants, such as palms and vines, and plants now found in colder climates, such as oak trees.

WHAT IS A MAMMAL?

Mammals are a diverse group of vertebrates that are now found in many different habitats. For example, whales and dolphins live in the oceans, beavers and otters live in rivers, moles and badgers live underground, elephants and deer live on land and bats fly through the skies. All mammals are warm-blooded and the females produce milk to feed their young. Most mammals give birth to live young, with the exception of a small group called monotremes, which lay eggs.

The **Riversleigh Platypus** is an extinct monotreme from Australia.

Diacodexis was one of the earliest relatives of pigs, deer and giraffes. It was the size of a squirrel and moved by leaping.

2 | *Around 65–28 MYA* PRIMATES SWING THROUGH THE TREES

Early primates probably benefited from the new forests and flowering plants. Evolving long arms and legs as well as fingers that could grasp, primates could leap around the treetops and snatch tasty flowers and fruit to eat.

Aegyptopithecus once lived in dense forests in what is now Egypt. It was the earliest member of a primate group that also includes the ancestor of humans.

Smilodectes was related to modern lemurs. It had sharp vision, making it good at detecting food and judging distances for jumping.

3 | *50–33 MYA* BACK TO THE WATER

Whales evolved from land mammals. We know this because their backbones don't bend from side to side as those of fishes do. Instead, whales move their tails up and down like running dogs. Here are some examples to show how they might have evolved:

A. *Pakicetus* was roughly the size of a goat and hunted along the water's edge. The shape of its skull suggests it was an ancestor of whales.

B. *Ambulocetus* (meaning 'walking whale') swam with webbed feet and a muscular tail. It also spent time on land, but would have found it difficult to walk far.

C. *Basilosaurus* lived entirely in water and had a tail fin, but also small back legs. It came to the surface to breathe air through nostrils similar to the blowhole found in modern whales.

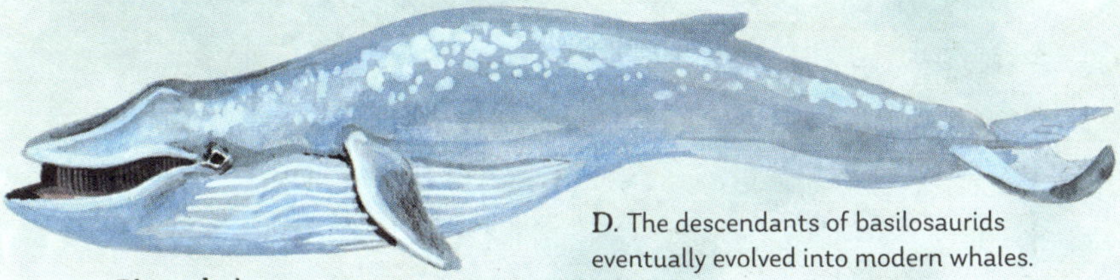

Blue whale

D. The descendants of basilosaurids eventually evolved into modern whales. Some modern whales still have small hip bones inside their bodies.

PIONEERING PEOPLE

Palaeontologist **Mary R. Dawson** (1931–2020) and her colleagues found fossil alligators, turtles and mammals on Ellesmere Island in Arctic Canada. This proved that the Arctic had been warm and ice-free over 50 MYA. These fossils provided evidence that there was once a land bridge between Europe and North America that allowed land animals to spread.

4 | *34–33 MYA* ANTARCTICA BECAME SURROUNDED BY WATER

Tectonic movements separated Australia and South America from Antarctica. Cold water circulated around Antarctica, allowing glaciers to form. Ocean currents spread north and the climate became cooler and drier. Many tropical species retreated from the polar regions.

358.9–298.9 MYA CARBONIFEROUS PERIOD

298.9–251.9 MYA PERMIAN PERIOD

251.9–201.3 MYA TRIASSIC PERIOD

201.3–145 MYA JURASSIC PERIOD

145–66 MYA CRETACEOUS PERIOD

66–23 MYA PALAEOGENE PERIOD

23–2.58 MYA NEOGENE PERIOD

2.58 MYA–Present QUATERNARY PERIOD

GRASSLANDS AND GRAZERS

NEOGENE PERIOD

During the Neogene Period, grasslands replaced the disappearing forests in many parts of the world. They became the centre of evolution for many new living things. Grasses were well adapted to the cool, dry climate and could withstand damage caused by wildfires and herds of animals grazing and trampling on them.

HOW HORSES EVOLVED

Horses first evolved in North American forests. They were small and had four toes on their front feet and three on their hind, making it easier to walk on the soft forest floor. When horses adapted to the new grasslands, they evolved longer legs and became larger. These changes allowed them to run quickly and flee from predators. Modern horses have single-toed feet with hooves that protect their toes when galloping on hard grasslands.

Many scientists think that *Hyracotherium* (55–45 MYA) was the first horse. It stood between 20–60 centimetres tall to the shoulder, depending on the species.

1 | *23.03–5.33 MYA* GREAT HORSE RACE

The number of horse species exploded in North America during the early Neogene to about 70 species of varying sizes. Horses used land bridges to move to other parts of the world, including South America, Europe, Africa and Asia. *Dinohippus* was the closest Neogene relative to modern horses and had already evolved hooves.

2 | *23.03 MYA onwards* GRASSLANDS CHANGED THE WORLD

Grasslands are open landscapes covered with grasses and wildflowers. They first occurred in central Asia and North America in the late Palaeogene and expanded in the Neogene. Grassland provided food for many new species. Animals such as horses and the ancestors of antelopes had special teeth that allowed them to eat the tough grass. Songbirds and rodents ate the seeds, flowers and insects. Grass grows from its base, so it could cope with the constant munching. Many predators, including some modern snakes, evolved here too, preying on the small grassland animals.

THE TIMELINE MYA means Million Years Ago | 4,600–4,000 MYA HADEAN EON | 4,000–2,500 MYA ARCHEAN EON | 2,500–538.8 MYA PROTEROZOIC EON | 538.8–485.4 MYA CAMBRIAN PERIOD | 485.4–443.8 MYA ORDOVICIAN PERIOD | 443.8–419.2 MYA SILURIAN PERIOD | 419.2–358.9 MYA DEVONIAN PERIOD

3 | *Around 23 MYA* THE AGE OF APES

Humans and other apes share a common ancestor that died out millions of years ago. We don't know exactly what this ancestor looked like, but it may have been similar to *Proconsul*, an ape-like animal that was abundant in Africa during the early to mid Neogene. *Proconsul* had a bigger brain than that of a monkey and lacked a tail.

PIONEERING PEOPLE

Mary D. Leakey (1913–1996) studied the origin of humans and our ancestors. When working in Kenya, she discovered the first fossil skull of *Proconsul*, which may have been one of the ancestors of humans and the other great apes.

4 | *18.6 MYA* ELEPHANTS MOVE TO EUROPE

A land bridge connecting Africa with Asia and Europe allowed animals to migrate between these areas. Asian animals, such as rhinos, moved to Africa, and elephant-like species, such as *Deinotherium giganteum*, dispersed from Africa to Asia and Europe.

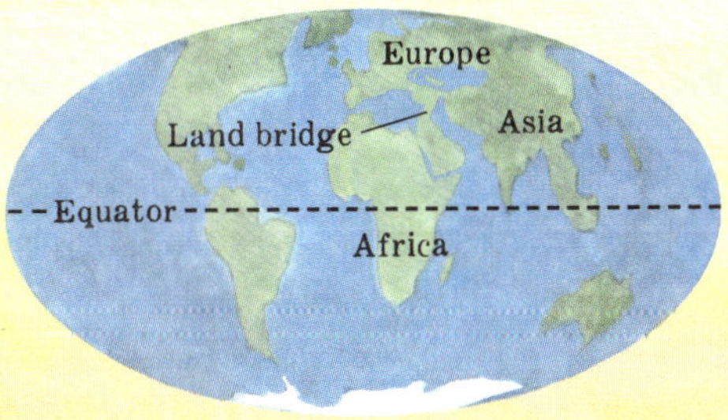

358.9–298.9 MYA CARBONIFEROUS PERIOD

298.9–251.9 MYA PERMIAN PERIOD

251.9–201.3 MYA TRIASSIC PERIOD

201.3–145 MYA JURASSIC PERIOD

145–66 MYA CRETACEOUS PERIOD

66–23 MYA PALAEOGENE PERIOD

23–2.58 MYA NEOGENE PERIOD

2.58 MYA–Present QUATERNARY PERIOD

THE SUCCESS OF BIRDS

Scientists and bird lovers alike have long been impressed by the beautiful and interesting characteristics of our feathered friends. Some birds have brightly coloured feathers, others have beautiful songs or impressive dance moves and some use their beaks in very clever ways. Birds have taught us a lot about evolution – from the ways in which they find food to how they choose their mates. They are also an evolutionary link to dinosaurs!

PIONEERING PEOPLE

Peter (1936–present) and **Rosemary Grant** (1936–present) have been studying evolution in action in Darwin's finches for more than 40 years. Along with their children, they have lived for many months at a time on a small, deserted Galápagos Island called Daphne Major.

The woodpecker finch has a narrow beak to pull insects from tree crevices. It can also use a cactus spine as a tool!

The cactus finch has a long, straight beak that it uses to feed on cactus pollen and nectar.

DARWIN'S FINCHES

While visiting the Galápagos Islands, Darwin made a collection of small birds that are now known as Darwin's finches. These finches represent about 13 different species in the Galápagos. Scientists believe that a single species arrived on these islands around 2–3 million years ago. Once there, the finches would have found new food sources. Finches with different variations would have had access to different food. Natural selection took advantage of any small variations and the birds developed different beak shapes. This process is called adaptive radiation. Finch populations probably became isolated from each other, perhaps as some flew to different islands. This meant that they evolved into many new species. Now, several species of finch can be found in the same area, each feeding on different food sources.

The large ground finch has an impressive, strong beak to crack hard seeds.

The sharp-beaked ground finch mainly feeds on seeds and insects. However, some of these finches also use their sharp beaks to drink the blood of other birds – they are known as vampire finches.

CHOOSING A MATE

Many animals choose their mates based on certain characteristics that they find attractive – this is called sexual selection. Sexual selection is an important driver for evolution. Animals with certain 'attractive' features or habits are more likely to be selected by a mate. They will then have young who will inherit their characteristics. Here are a few characteristics and behaviours that male birds can have that allow them to really stand out from the crowd.

Blue manakins impressing a female

Getting in the groove

Male blue manakin birds impress females with their organised dance moves. They can spend years perfecting their routines, ready to perform as a group when the time is right. The males take turns flying over one another in the hope of encouraging the watching female to mate with the lead male dancer.

A peacock and its colourful tail

Getting attention!

The peacock's tail evolved because of sexual selection. Females, called peahens, find males with long, pretty tails very attractive. So, peacocks with fancy tails are more successful in finding a mate and fathering lots of young who can inherit the long-tailed characteristic. Peahens, on the other hand, have brown feathers that allow them to remain hidden and avoid predators while looking after their eggs.

Common nightingale

Singing superstars

Birds can sing for several reasons, such as to mark their territory or attract a mate. The male nightingale's song is particularly beautiful and is an example of both of these things. Female nightingales will often select a male singer with an especially complex song. Research has shown that these males tend to make good fathers as they provide more food for their chicks.

Taking to the stage

The male satin bowerbird builds a structure, called a bower, which he decorates with flowers. He dances back and forth across his stage, while puffing up his feathers and buzzing. His aim is to attract a mate. If the bird lives near humans, the floor of the bower might also be decorated with colourful objects, such as bottle tops and children's hair ties!

ARE DINOSAURS EXTINCT?

Birds are an evolutionary link to dinosaurs. Modern birds are descended from dinosaurs and most palaeontologists agree that birds are actually a type of dinosaur. Shortly after Darwin and Wallace presented their theory of evolution, a bird-like fossil from the Jurassic was found. It was called *Archaeopteryx*. It had characteristics of both birds and dinosaurs: dinosaur-like claws, teeth and a bony tail as well as bird-like wings and feathers. It offered an exciting link between birds and dinosaurs.

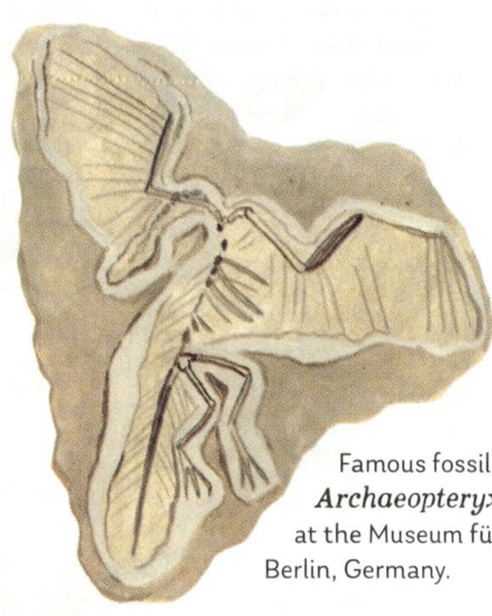

Famous fossil of *Archaeopteryx* that is kept at the Museum für Naturkunde Berlin, Germany.

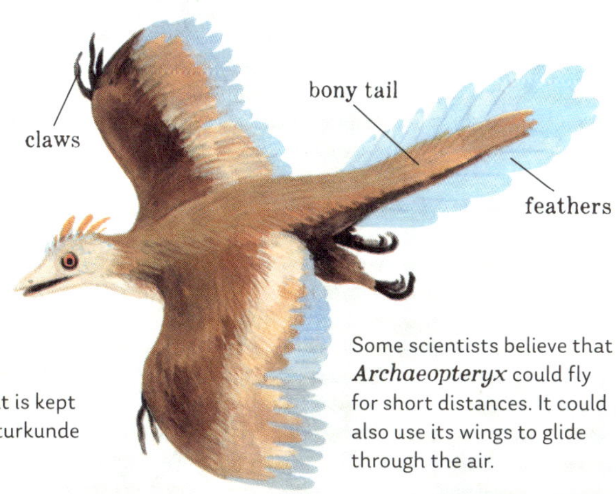

Some scientists believe that *Archaeopteryx* could fly for short distances. It could also use its wings to glide through the air.

EVOLUTION OF HUMANS

NEOGENE AND QUATERNARY PERIODS

Several species of humans existed in the past. *Homo sapiens*, our species, is the only one still alive today. It is still unclear how all the various species were related, but we do know that our closest living relatives are chimpanzees and bonobos.

PIONEERING PEOPLE

Berhane Asfaw (1954–present) discovered a 160,000-year-old skull, one of the oldest fossils of *Homo sapiens*. He also unearthed many other human fossils that suggest humans originated in Ethiopia.

1 | *4.4–2.95 MYA* ANCESTOR OF MODERN HUMANS

The discovery of a fossil that was later named Lucy helped to shape our understanding of human history. Lucy belonged to an extinct group called *Australopithecus*. She had characteristics of modern humans (she walked upright) and our ape-like ancestors (she had long arms for climbing trees). Walking upright was an important evolutionary step. It gave early humans a better view of their surroundings, allowing them to spot predators. It also freed up their hands so that they could carry tools, food and their young.

2 | *Since 3.3 MYA or earlier* TOOL MAKING

Early humans (perhaps including *Australopithecus*) crafted flint stone tools. These knife-sharp tools allowed our ancestors to eat a wide range of foods, including meat and bone marrow.

3 | *About 2.8–1.4 MYA* ONE OF THE EARLIEST HUMAN SPECIES

Homo habilis lived in East and South Africa and had a bigger brain than *Australopithecus*. Due to the cooler and drier climate, fruits that were once available became rare. Meat became an essential part of *Homo habilis*'s diet.

4 | *About 2 MYA–110,000 years ago* OUT OF AFRICA

Homo erectus had similar proportions and were a similar size to modern humans. They were also smart. Fossil remains have been found in East Africa, parts of Asia and Europe, so it is clear *Homo erectus* migrated far and wide. It looks as if they crossed short stretches of open ocean and may have even built rafts.

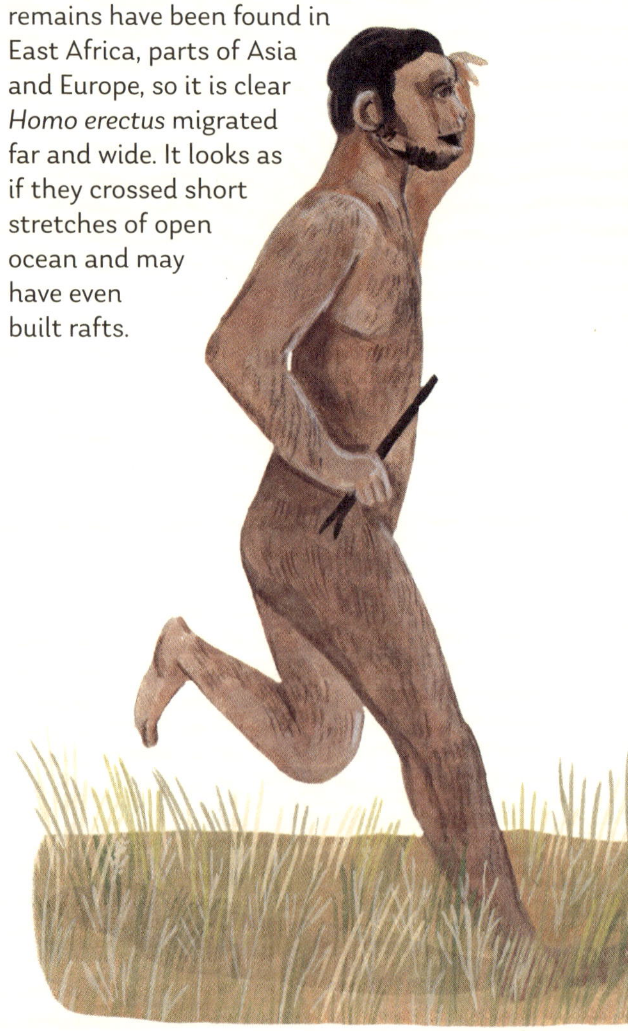

THE TIMELINE MYA means Million Years Ago	4,600–4,000 MYA HADEAN EON	4,000–2,500 MYA ARCHEAN EON	2,500–538.8 MYA PROTEROZOIC EON	538.8–485.4 MYA CAMBRIAN PERIOD	485.4–443.8 MYA ORDOVICIAN PERIOD	443.8–419.2 MYA SILURIAN PERIOD	419.2–358.9 MYA DEVONIAN PERIOD

5 | *About 1 MYA* FIRST CHEFS

The ability to use fire meant our ancestors could cook their food. Cooking makes food easier to digest, giving humans extra energy and nutrients. This energy was, in part, used to support a larger brain. Fire also provided people with a source of heat and light at nighttime. This not only gave them a place to gather, but also provided protection against wild animals.

7 | *About 300,000 years ago* THE FIRST MODERN HUMANS (THAT'S US!)

Homo sapiens are believed to have evolved in Africa. Our smart brains helped us plan, solve problems and communicate. This enabled us to deal with a constantly changing climate and environment. Modern humans have since populated the rest of the world.

6 | *About 400,000–30,000 years ago* *HOMO NEANDERTHALENSIS*

Neanderthals lived in Europe and southwest Asia. They wore animal skin clothes, made necklaces and ivory carvings and created cave paintings. Neanderthals and modern humans (*Homo sapiens*) lived alongside one another and bred with each other. It's most likely that *Homo sapiens* played a role in the extinction of Neanderthals.

A TIME OF INVENTION

Both Neanderthals and early *Homo sapiens* lived by hunting, fishing and gathering wild plants. They created tools that helped them flourish in different parts of the world. By 40,000 years ago our ancestors were also creating works of art and playing music.

Sculptures
This lion man sculpture appears as half animal, half human. It is about 40,000 years old and from Germany.

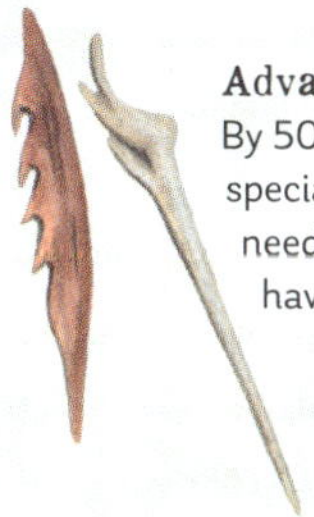

Musical instruments
This flute was made from the wing bone of a bird. It is 35,000 years old and from Germany.

Cave paintings
Some cave paintings from France show mammoths and woolly rhinos. They are about 35,000 years old.

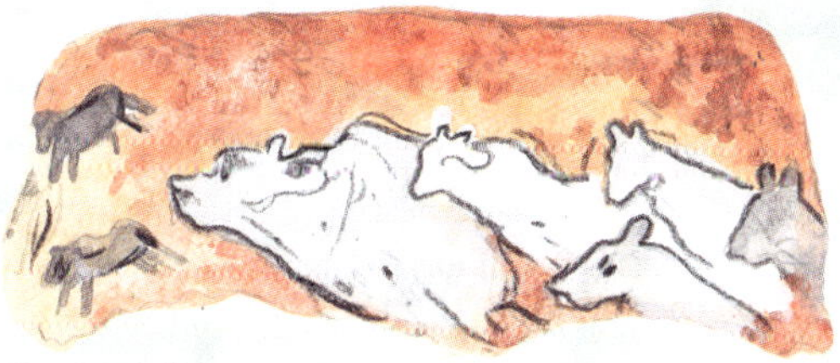

Advanced tools
By 50,000 years ago humans were crafting many specialised tools, such as fish hooks and sewing needles out of shell, ivory and bone. These artefacts have been found in many locations around the world.

Map
This map was carved onto mammoth tusk. It is 27,000 years old and from the Czech Republic.

Stone points
The oldest evidence of arrows are 64,000 years old and from South Africa.

HUMANS CHANGE THEIR WORLD

QUATERNARY PERIOD

For hundreds of thousands of years, our ancestors were hunter-gatherers and found all their food in the wild. That is, until they started to farm. This might have begun by accident when people noticed seeds growing. Plants were selected and bred because they could easily be grown or were tasty. Animals were also chosen for being strong or tame. This artificial selection – when breeders choose characteristics in plants or animals that benefit humans – is also known as domestication. Farming emerged in many areas around the world at different times. Rice was first farmed in China, and tomatoes, potatoes, corn and cacao were first farmed in the Americas.

CROP COUSINS

Crops continue to evolve as breeders select different variations to suit changes in growing conditions and trends in what people eat. Because of this selective breeding, many wild relatives of crop plants look very different to their domesticated cousins. For example, the wild mustard plant looks quite different to the vegetables that have been artificially selected from it.

1 | *Up to 40,000 years ago* BECOMING HUMANS' BEST FRIENDS

Dogs are thought to have been the first domesticated animals. All dogs evolved from wild wolves. It is possible that wolves might have hung around humans to steal food, or maybe humans cared for and trained orphaned wolf pups. Humans selected wolves with certain characteristics, such as those that were fast runners, smart or gentle, and bred from them. Dogs became important members of hunter-gatherer communities. Later, they helped people in many ways, such as herding and guarding sheep.

2 | *12,000–6,000 years ago* EARLY FARMING

Some scientists believe that humans first tried growing plants about 23,000 years ago. But farming really took off around 12,000 years ago. In an area called the Fertile Crescent in the Middle East, people farmed plants and animals, including wheat, lentils, goats, cattle and pigs. Gradually, some people gave up the mobile hunter-gatherer lifestyle and settled into permanent homes. Villages and cities developed and food and goods were stored and traded. Writing was developed to keep track of goods that were bought and sold.

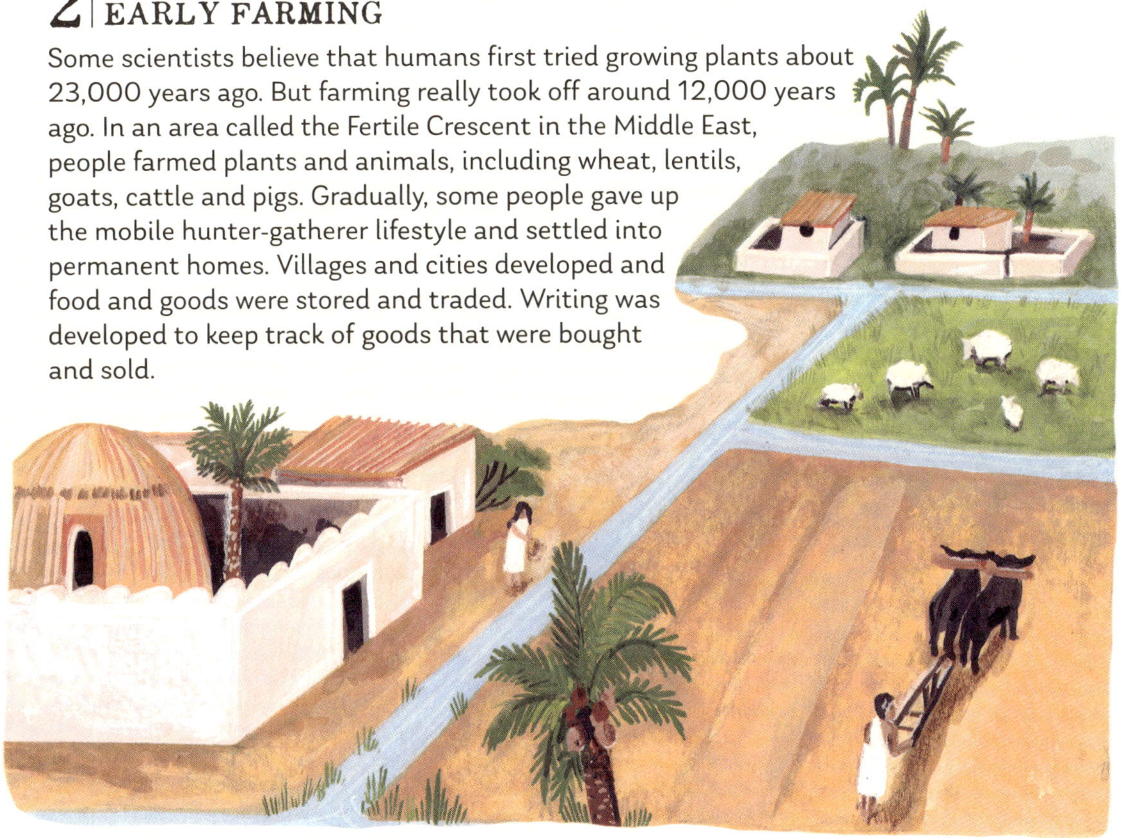

3 | *About 7,500–5,000 years ago* FANCY FABRIC

Around this time, people in different parts of the world were experimenting with making fabrics out of flax, wool and cotton. But farmers in China were the first to domesticate silk moth caterpillars and make silk. These caterpillars eat mulberry leaves and when they are fully grown, they spin cocoons. The farmers collect these cocoons, unwind the fine fibres and weave them into delicate silk fabric.

PIONEERING PEOPLE

Thomas Phillip Lecky (1904–1994) bred different types of cattle and developed a dairy breed that he called 'Jamaica Hope'. This breed is adapted to the tropical and hilly conditions on the Caribbean island of Jamaica: it has strong legs, can cope with the heat and is resistant to tropical ticks.

4 | *About 2,200–1,300 years ago* THE SILK ROAD

Silk and other goods were traded throughout Asia and Europe along a network of routes called the Silk Road. The use of domesticated plants and animals spread, and knowledge and innovations were shared between different cultures. Trade routes also developed elsewhere in the world at about the same time.

HUMAN-MADE

QUATERNARY PERIOD

In the 18th and 19th centuries many things changed in the human world. New machines were invented and goods were produced more quickly and cheaply than ever before. Steel production increased, trains and cars were developed and skyscrapers were built.

1 | *18th and 19th centuries* MAKING MORE AND BUILDING HIGHER

During the Industrial Revolution, many factories were driven by steam engines, which were powered by coal. Coal is a type of fossil fuel and burning it (and other fossil fuels) released greenhouse gases into the air. This also caused polluting substances to leak into the water and soil. The pollution had negative and far-reaching effects on our planet. It also affected the evolution of some living things.

2 | *1800s* THE PEPPERED MOTH

The peppered moth is a great example of how human activity can affect evolution. In some industrial areas of the UK, air pollution was so bad that trees became darkened with black soot from coal smoke. Local populations of peppered moths adapted to this change.

A. Peppered moths are typically light grey with dark speckles. They perfectly match the bark of silver birch trees, which means they are camouflaged so hungry birds can't easily see them.

B. In the mid 1800s a variation of the peppered moth with much darker wings was first discovered. These moths were camouflaged in industrial areas where the trees were covered with soot.

C. The pale moths were more successful in the unpolluted countryside. In these areas, the birds spotted and ate the dark moths and the pale moths survived.

D. In the polluted industrial areas, the dark peppered moths became more successful. The birds spotted and ate the pale moths. The best-suited moths survived in each environment and their offspring inherited their wing colour. This shows how natural selection can lead to changes within populations, even when caused by humans.

3 | *Today* CITY LIFE

On average, more than four human babies are born every second. Human populations are dramatically increasing and more than half of us now live in towns and cities. The building of cities and roads destroys many natural habitats. But these new urban environments can present opportunities as well as challenges. Some species have been driven to extinction by these difficulties, but others have evolved in surprising ways to cope with city life.

The **crested anole lizard** from Puerto Rico lives in both cities and nearby forests. City-dwelling lizards have more scales than their forest relatives. They also have longer legs, which allows them to quickly move from place to place in the busy city.

EVOLUTION OF VIRUSES

Humans can sometimes be infected by viruses that originated in wild animals. When humans and wild animals come into contact with each other, viruses can be transferred. This contact can happen when humans destroy animals' habitats, or hunt, capture or eat wild animals. Viruses evolve and can reproduce and mutate rapidly, which causes variations. Some variations allow them to be more successful in their struggle for existence. For example, the virus that causes COVID-19 evolved to become highly infectious, which allowed it to spread quickly through the human population.

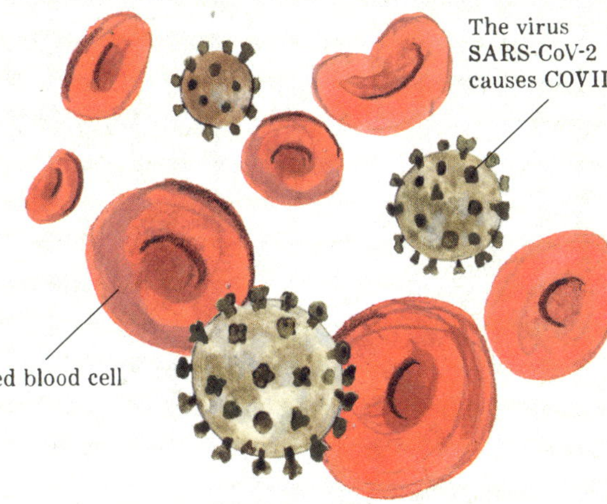

PIONEERING PEOPLE

Uğur Şahin (1965–present) and **Özlem Türeci** (1967–present) invented one of the first vaccinations to protect people against COVID-19. They won an award from the German government for their achievement.

4 | *Today* HUMAN-MADE CLIMATE CRISIS

Earth's weather is becoming more unpredictable and in many places temperatures are rising. Most scientists believe that this is largely due to the increased amount of greenhouse gases in the atmosphere. Ice in the polar regions and glaciers are melting, leading to a rise in sea levels and flooding along the coasts. More seawater is evaporating, forming clouds that make intense rainstorms. Elsewhere, droughts and wildfires occur. There is evidence that some living things are already adapting to the climate crisis. Any that can't adapt will have to migrate or they will die out. But humans have a chance to slow down this change and protect our planet for future generations.

Warmer spring weather, caused by the climate crisis, has made a population of **red squirrels** in Canada give birth nearly three weeks earlier than they did ten years ago.

THE FUTURE

What does the future hold for the evolution of living things? It is impossible to predict. But one thing is for sure: as long as there is life, there will be evolution.

Earth is now in the midst of the sixth mass extinction. This is being caused by humans, so our actions will determine the future of life on Earth. The better we understand evolution, the better we can protect our planet.

By engaging with nature we can begin to appreciate it and work out how to protect it in the future. This may be as simple as going for a walk, planting a tree or learning more about the living things we share our planet with.

PIONEERING PEOPLE

There are lots of smart, hardworking, pioneering people from all over the world who are trying to understand what's happening to the planet and make things better. If we work together, we can save our planet's rich nature and guide humans towards a more sustainable future. The time to act is now. Perhaps the next pioneering person could be you?

Faysal Bibi (1980–present) is a scientist who studies Neogene and Quaternary fossils in Africa. Faysal and his team look at the relationships between animals to see how they respond to changes in the environment. Faysal aims to use this information to help predict how animals will cope with changes in the future and to work out how to protect them.

David Attenborough (1926–present) is an English biologist, nature documentary maker and television presenter. He has devoted his life to sharing the wonders of the natural world and now actively campaigns for nature conservation.

Jadav Payeng (1963–present) lives on Majuli, the world's largest river island in northeast India. As a 16-year-old, he started to plant one tree every day to try to repair the bare soil caused by severe droughts. More than 40 years later, his forest covers an area the size of 15 football stadiums and attracts many birds, elephants and other wildlife.

Fatemah Alzelzela (1996–present) started a recycling initiative called Eco Star in Kuwait. Eco Star takes recyclable waste from homes, schools and businesses and exchanges it for trees and plants. Since launching in early 2019, Eco Star has recycled more than 130 tonnes of metal, paper and plastic, and lots of trees have been planted!

Wangari Maathai (1940–2011) was the founder of The Green Belt Movement in Kenya. The organisation aims to re-grow forests and prevent the land from turning into desert. More than 30 million trees have been planted so far. Wangari has said: 'When we plant trees, we plant the seeds of peace and hope.'

Greta Thunberg (2003–present) started a global movement known as Fridays for Future. At the age of 15, she skipped school to protest in front of the Swedish government building. Her goal was to draw attention to the climate crisis and force politicians to take action. Greta's idea spread around the world and since then millions of young people have joined her to protest for a better future.

Helena Gualinga (2002–present) is a member of the Kichwa people of Sarayaku, an indigenous community in Ecuador. She campaigns for the protection of the Amazon rainforest and the people who live there.

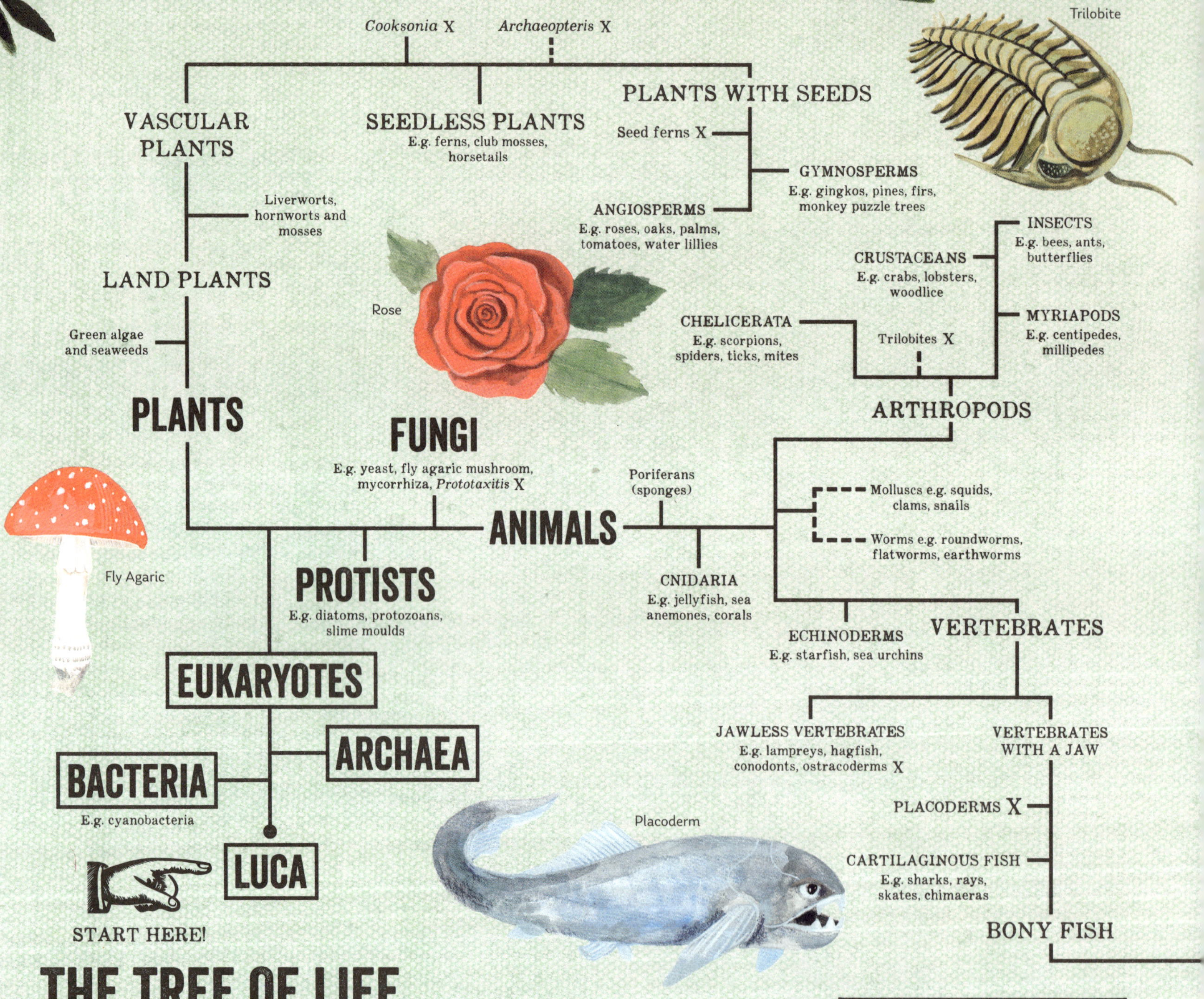

THE TREE OF LIFE

All living things are related to each other and share a common ancestor called LUCA, which stands for the Last Universal Common Ancestor. Many scientists believe that LUCA was a microscopic organism that lived about 4 billion years ago. Traditionally, scientists have used a diagram called the tree of life to show the main groups of living things and the order in which they evolved.

KEY

----	– link still under discussion
X	– Extinct
Italicised	– Scientific name
E.g.	– For example

CALL ME *T. REX* FOR SHORT

Scientists give every living thing a unique double name, often in Latin or Greek. The first part of the name refers to the genus, which is the group of closely related species that the living thing belongs to. The second part is the species. In the name *Tyrannosaurus rex*, for example, *Tyrannosaurus* refers to a group of dinosaurs called theropods and *rex* is the species name. Together *Tyrannosaurus rex* gives this fearsome dinosaur a unique scientific name that can be shortened to *T. rex*.

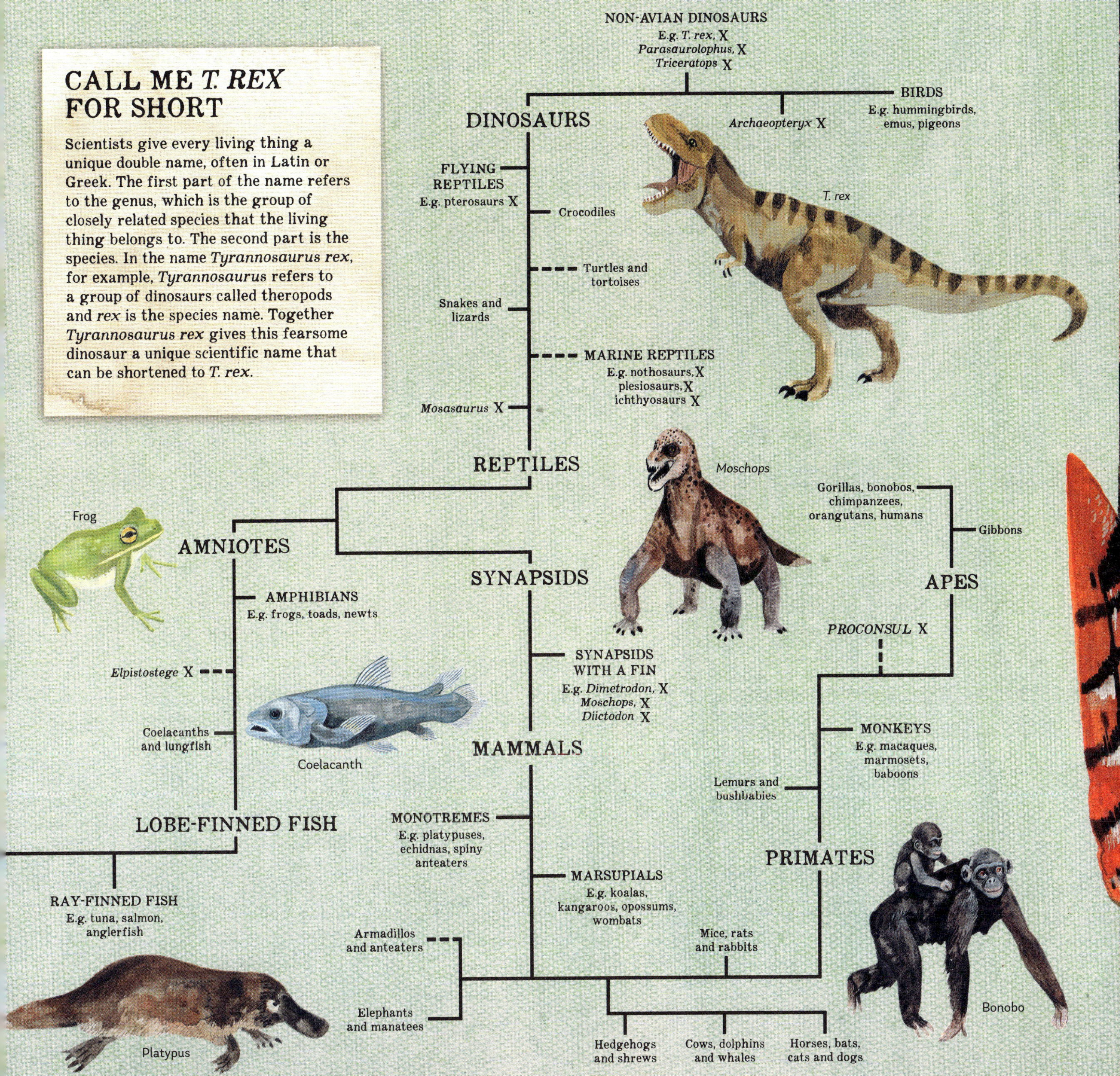

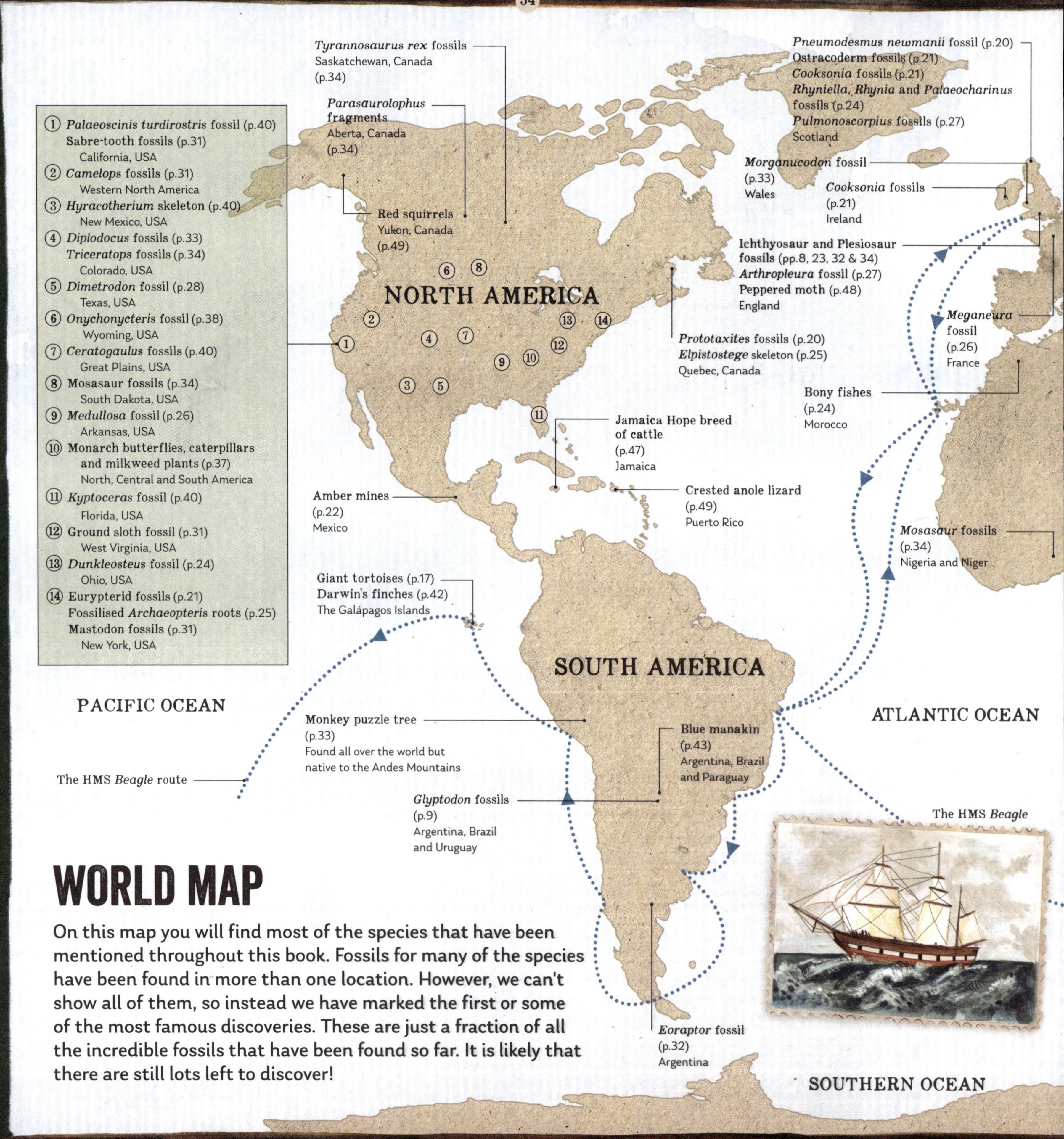

WORLD MAP

On this map you will find most of the species that have been mentioned throughout this book. Fossils for many of the species have been found in more than one location. However, we can't show all of them, so instead we have marked the first or some of the most famous discoveries. These are just a fraction of all the incredible fossils that have been found so far. It is likely that there are still lots left to discover!

ARCTIC OCEAN
Calamites and *Psaronius* fossils (p.26)
Delitzschala fossil (p.26)
Eudibamus specimen (p.28)
Nothosaur fossil (p.32)
Eomys fossil (p.38)
Archaeopteryx fossil (p.43)
Homo neanderthalensis fossils (p.45)
Germany
Scutosaurus fossils
(p.28)
Ural Mountains, Russia
EUROPE
Ginkgophyte fossils
(pp.29 & 33)
Fergana Valley, Uzbekistan,
Tajikistan and Kyrgyzstan
Common nightingale
(p. 43)
Migrates from Europe to
Subsaharan Africa in winter
Pterosaur fossils
(p. 34)
Italian Alps
Voltziales fossils
(p.29)
Mongolia
Fertile Crescent
(p.47)
Parts of Iraq, Syria, Lebanon, Jordan,
Palestine, Israel, Egypt, Turkey and Iran
ASIA
Hallucigenia, trilobite, *Pikaia*, conodont,
eocrinoid, *Opabinia* and *Anomalocaris*
fossils (p.19)
Cycad fossils (pp.29 & 33)
Stegosaurus fossil (p.33)
Silk moth caterpillars (p.47)
China
Deinotherium
giganteum
(p.41)
Crete, Greece
Paraceratherium fossils (p.38)
Pakicetus and *Ambulocetus* fossils (p.39)
Pakistan
Aegyptopithecus fossils and
Basilosaurus skeleton
(p.39)
Egypt
Glossopteris fossil
(p.29)
India
AFRICA
Lucy, the *Australopithecus*
skeleton (p.44)
Homo sapiens (pp.44 & 45)
Ethiopia
Blue peacock
(p.43)
Native to India and Sri Lanka
The Wallace Line
INDIAN OCEAN
Proconsul fossils
(p.41)
Kenya
PACIFIC OCEAN
Diictodon fossils
(p.28)
Zambia
Giraffatitan fossil (p.33)
Homo habilis fossils (p.44)
Tanzania
Homo erectus fossils
(p.44)
Java, Indonesia
Ediacaran fossils
(p.19)
Namibia
Ordovician fossils
(p.20)
Canning Basin,
Western Australia
Riversleigh
Platypus fossil
(p.38)
Queensland,
Australia
Coelurosauravus fossils (p.28)
Madagascan Star Orchid (p.36)
Madagascar
AUSTRALIA
Satin bowerbird
(p.43)
East coast of
Australia
Moschops fossils (p.28)
Procynosuchus fossils (p.29)
South Africa
Ammonoid fossils
(p.21)
Found all over the world, including Antarctica
Ediacaran fossils
(p.19)
Ediacara Hills, Australia
ANTARCTICA

GLOSSARY

Here is a list of important words used in this book and their scientific definitions. Words in bold are defined within the glossary.

Adapt
When living things, or **populations** of living things, change in order to suit the environment or situation in which they live.

Adaptive radiation
The process by which living things evolve from a shared **ancestor** into new species.

Amphibians
A group of cold-blooded living things with backbones. Adult amphibians have lungs to breathe air, while their young have gills and live in water. Examples are frogs, toads, newts and salamanders.

Ancestor
A living thing from which a species (or an individual) is descended. Your great-great grandmother is one of your ancestors.

Angiosperms
Flowering plants that produce seeds, which are protected in fruit.

Archaea
One of the three main groups of living things. Archaea are single-celled microscopic organisms and are similar to (but not the same as) **bacteria**. Together with bacteria, they form a group called **prokaryotes**.

Arthropods
A group of living things that includes insects, crabs and spiders and have at least three pairs of jointed legs and a hard **exoskeleton**.

Artificial selection
When humans select and breed certain plants or animals because they have characteristics or features that are desirable for human use.

Atmosphere
The mixture of gases that surround a planet.

Atom
The basic building blocks of all matter found in the universe.

Bacteria
A large group of microscopic single-celled living things that do not have a nucleus.

Biodiversity
The variety of living things in the world or in a specific **habitat**.

Cartilage
Soft connective tissue found in the bodies of many animals. Some animals, such as sharks, have skeletons made of cartilage rather than bone.

Characteristics
The features of a living thing. Some characteristics can be seen, for example fur or eye colour. Some characteristics are to do with the way living things behave, such as the way they hunt or live together.

Chloroplast
The green part of a plant cell that uses sunlight to create energy for the plant during **photosynthesis**.

Climate
The usual weather conditions that take place in a particular area over a long period of time.

Coevolution
Where two or more species evolve together and each affects how the other evolves.

Colony
Where members of the same species of living things live together in a group. Plants, animals, bacteria and fungi can live in colonies.

Continent
A large continuous piece of land on the surface of Earth. There are currently seven continents: Asia, Australia, Africa, Antarctica, Europe, North America and South America.

Crop
A plant or fungi that is cultivated and grown for food, such as rice or wheat, or for other purposes like making fabric, such as cotton.

Decay
The process by which living things, or parts of living things (like leaves from trees), rot due to the action of bacteria or fungi.

Descendant
A living thing that has come from a known **ancestor**. For example, birds are descendants of dinosaurs and a child is a descendant of its grandparents.

DNA (Deoxyribonucleic acid)
A large molecule that carries a living thing's genetic information and is inherited from an individual's biological parents. Genetic information gives a living thing its special characteristics.

Domestication
The process by which wild animals and plants are selected and tamed or bred by humans. This is the same as **artificial selection**. This causes the living things to change to benefit humans, for example making them easier to farm or able to live with humans.

Echinoderms
A group of **invertebrate** marine animals. Echinoderms often have a hard or spiny covering. Examples are sea urchins, sea stars and sea cucumbers.

Embryo
A living thing that is growing and developing before being born, hatching or germinating (which is what plants do when they start to put out shoots).

Environment
The surroundings of a living thing, including the conditions and interactions that the living thing needs to survive.

Equator
An imaginary line that goes around the centre of Earth like a belt. It separates the northern and southern hemispheres.

Eukaryote
An organism whose cell or cells have DNA enclosed in a **nucleus**. Animals, plants and fungi are eukaryotes.

Evolution
Evolution is the way that living things change over time. **Natural selection** is one of the mechanisms of evolution.

Exoskeleton
The hard outer covering that protects the soft insides of many **invertebrates**.

Extinction
When a whole species of living thing dies out or disappears completely. Living things can sometimes be extinct in the wild but still alive in captivity, or be described as locally extinct where they have died out in just one area.

Fossil
The remains or traces of a once-living thing. Fossils are usually preserved in rock.

Fossil fuels
Substances, such as coal, oil or natural gas, which are burned to get energy. They were formed by the partial decomposition of dead plants and animals that were buried in the earth.

Fungi
A group of organisms that produce spores and get their energy from decomposing organic material. Fungi can live in soil, water and air, and some live in or on the bodies of other living things. Some species of fungi produce mushrooms.

Genetic
Relating to genes – the information carried in DNA and that provides the code for how a living thing grows and develops.

Geology
The science that focuses on the structure, processes and history of Earth.

Glacier
A large mass of ice that has built up over many years from snow falling and not melting. Glaciers slowly flow downhill.

Gravity
A force that pulls objects towards each other. Gravity keeps most things from floating off the surface of Earth and keeps the planets in our solar system in orbit around the Sun.

Greenhouse effect
A natural process that keeps Earth warm. **Greenhouse gases** such as carbon dioxide and methane in Earth's atmosphere trap heat that rises up from Earth's surface and stops it from escaping out into space.

Greenhouse gases
Gases that trap heat in Earth's atmosphere. Examples are water vapour, carbon dioxide and methane.

Gymnosperm
A large group of plants whose seeds are most often carried in cones rather than fruit. Examples are pine trees and gingkos.

Habitat
The place and surrounding conditions that a living thing needs to survive.

Indigenous
A living thing that is found living or growing naturally in an area. For example, Galápagos giant tortoises are indigenous to the Galápagos Islands. Humans can also be described as being indigenous to a particular area.

Inheritance
A process by which characteristics can be passed onto the next generation, such as how hair colour can be passed on from biological parent to child.

Invertebrates
Animals that do not have a backbone, such as snails and jellyfish.

Isolated
When a species, population or individual living thing is separated from other individuals belonging to the same species, preventing them from breeding together.

Land bridge
A strip of land that joins two larger areas of land that are mostly separated by sea.

Mantle
One of Earth's layers that is made of mostly solid rock and is located between the outer crust and the core.

Monotremes
A small group of mammals that lay eggs rather than give birth to living young. Examples are the platypus and echidna.

Mutation
A change in **DNA** that can take place by chance. Mutations can be inherited.

Natural selection
A process that leads to evolution. Individuals that have **characteristics** that make them better suited than others to their environment, survive and have healthy young. The young inherit characteristics from their parents. Natural selection can lead to the formation of new species.

Nucleus
A part of a cell that is surrounded by a membrane and contains genetic material, such as **DNA**.

Nutrients
Substances that help living things to grow and thrive.

Organic
A substance containing carbon, which usually comes from a living thing.

Organism
A living thing.

Palaeontologist
A scientist who studies the history of life by examining fossils.

Photosynthesis
The process by which plants and some bacteria produce sugar and oxygen, using carbon dioxide, water and sunlight.

Pollen
A tiny grain that is produced by plants and contains the male reproductive material. Pollen is needed for **pollination** to take place in order for a plant to produce seeds.

Pollination
When **pollen** is transported to a plant by wind or by a pollinator (such as a bee). In the flower, the pollen fertilises the plant's egg cell and a seed develops.

Population
A group of living things belonging to the same species that live close enough to one another to be able to breed together.

Predator
An animal that hunts or catches other animals for food.

Prey
Animals that are hunted by other animals.

Prokaryotes
Microscopic living things that lack a **nucleus** in their cell. Examples are **bacteria** and **archaea**.

Radioactive
Relating to materials that are made of certain chemical elements that change over time and release a form of energy that can be harmful to living things.

Reproduction
The process by which living things produce their young.

Scavenger
An animal that eats the remains of animals that have died naturally or that predators have killed.

Sediment
Solid materials that settle to the bottom of a body of water, such as a lake or ocean.

Sexual selection
A driver for evolution that explains why some animals have **characteristics** or behaviours that help them to secure a mate. An example is the peacock's colourful tail. The peahens (females) choose the peacocks (males) with the most colourful tails to mate with.

Species
A group of closely related living things that share common features. Members of a species can breed together and have healthy young who can also reproduce.

Spores
Tiny grains produced by fungi and some plants (such as ferns, mosses, horsetails) in which their **genetic** material is contained. Plant spores grow into structures that have both male and female cells on which a new plant forms.

Synapsids
A large group of animals that includes all mammals and their extinct ancestors. Synapsids first evolved in the Carboniferous Period and formed many new species in the Permian Period.

Tectonic plates
Large sections of Earth's crust that sit on the **mantle**. Tectonic plates move slowly across Earth's surface. When they collide they form mountains. The areas near the edges of tectonic plates often have volcanic activity and earthquakes.

Theory
A scientific idea about how something works that is supported by evidence.

Variation
Differences that are found between living things within the same species. For example, individuals of a species of snail might have variations in the colour of their shells.

Vascular plants
Plants that have internal tubes that transport water and nutrients to different parts of the plant. Vascular plants include most land plants, except for mosses, liverworts and hornworts.

Vertebrate
A group of animals that have a backbone. They include fish, amphibians, reptiles, birds and mammals.

INDEX

A

adaptations 10, 11, 13, 17, 28
adaptive radiation 42
advantage 13, 26, 42
Aegyptopithecus 39
Agrawal, Anurag 37
Albedo Effect 30
Alvarez, Luis and Walter 35
Alzelzela, Fatemah 51
Amazon rainforest 6, 51
amber 22
Ambulocetus 39
ammonites 23
amphibians 27
Anamalocaris 19
angiosperms 35
Anning, Mary 8, 23
Antarctica 39
apes 41
Archaeopteris 25
Archaeopteryx 43
Archean Eon 14
armadillos 9
Arthropleura 27
arthropods 27
Asaro, Frank 35
Asfaw, Berhane 44
asteroids 14, 15, 35
atmosphere 15, 27, 35
Attenborough, David 51
Australopithecus 44

B

bacteria 15, 18, 22
Basilosaurus 39
Beagle, HMS 8
Bibi, Faysal 51
biodiversity 6
birds 35, 42–3
bony fish 24
bony plates 33
bowerbirds 43
brachiopods 20

C

Cambrian Explosion 19
Cambrian Period 18, 19
carbon dioxide 15, 25, 27, 30, 31
Carboniferous Period 26–7, 28
caterpillars 37
cave paintings 45
characteristics 8, 10, 11, 43
Chinsamy-Turan, Anusuya 33
chloroplasts 18
climate change 13, 16, 20, 25, 27, 28, 29, 32, 39, 49
  causes of 30–1
climate crisis 31, 49, 51
coal 26, 27, 48
Coelurosauravus 28
coevolution 36–7
comets 14
competition 19, 37
conodonts 19
conservation 51
continents 15, 16, 17, 27, 38
Cooksonia 21
core, Earth's 14
COVID-19 49
Cretaceous Period 16, 34–5
crops 46
crust, Earth's 14, 15
currents, ocean 16, 39
Cuvier, Georges 8
cyanobacteria 15, 18
cycads 29

D

Darwin, Charles 8–9, 10, 15, 17, 36, 42, 43
Darwin, Erasmus 8
Dawson, Mary R. 39
Deinotherium giganteum 41
Delitzschala 26
Devonian Period 24–5
Diacodexis 38
diatoms 23
Diictodon 28
Dimetrodon 28
Dinohippus 40
dinosaurs 32–3, 34, 35, 42, 43, 53
Diplodocus 33
DNA 11, 12
dogs 46
domestication 46
Dunkleosteus 24

E

Earth
  climate change 30–1
  future of life on 50
  geological periods 14–16, 18–21, 24–9, 32–5, 38–41, 44–9
earthquakes 16, 32
Ediacaran Period 19
eggs, amniotic 26, 38
elephants 41
Elpistostege 25
environment 10, 11, 13, 51
eocrinoids 19
Eomys 38
Eoraptor 32
Eryops 27
Eudibamus 28
eukaryotes 18
existence, struggle for 10, 11, 12
extinction 13, 19, 20, 31, 32, 35, 49, 50

F

fabrics 47
farming 46, 47
Fertile Crescent 47
finches, Darwin's 42
fire 45
fish 21, 24–5
flight 26, 34, 43
flowers 34, 35, 36–7, 38, 39
footprints 22
forests 38, 39
fossil fuels 31, 48
fossils 9, 17, 20, 22–3, 29, 39, 43, 51, 54–5
fruit 35
fungi 20, 24

G

Galápagos Islands 17, 42
Gaulinga, Helena 51
Giraffatitan 33
giraffes 8
glaciers 27, 28, 39, 49
global warming 29, 32
Glyptodon 9
Gondwana 16, 17, 20
Grant, Peter and Rosemary 32
graptolites 20
grasslands 40–1
gravity 14
grazers 40–1
Great Oxidation Event 15
greenhouse gases 15, 30, 31, 49
gymnosperms 29

H

Hadean Eon 14
Hallucigenia 19
Henslow, John Stevens 8
Herschel, John Frederick William 8
Homo erectus 44
Homo habilis 44
Homo neanderthalensis 45
Homo sapiens 44, 45
horses 40
horsetails 26, 27
human activity 31, 48–9, 50
human evolution 41, 44–5
Humboldt, Alexander von 8
hunter-gatherers 45, 46
Hyracotherium 40

I

ice
  Albedo Effect 30
  melting 49
ice age 15
ichthyosaurs 32
Industrial Revolution 48
inheritance 8, 10, 11, 12, 43
insects
  giant 27
  pollination 35, 36–7
island populations 17, 42
isolation 13, 17, 42

J

jawed fish 21
Jurassic Period 16, 32–3, 43

K

Kuratani, Shigeru 21

L

Lamarck, Jean-Baptiste 8
land bridges 38, 40, 41
Laurasia 16
Leakey, Mary D. 41

leaves 25, 35
Lecky, Thomas Philip 47
legs, dinosaur 32
life on Earth 14, 50
Linnean Society 9
lithosphere 16
live young 38
lobe-finned fish 24, 25
LUCA (Last Universal Common Ancestor) 52
Lyell, Charles 8, 15
Lyell, Mary Horner 15

M

Maathai, Wangari 51
magma 14, 15
Malthus, Thomas 8
mammals 29, 33, 38–9
manakins, blue 43
mantle 14
Margulis, Lynn 18
mass extinctions
  End-Permian 28, 29, 32
  End-Triassic 32
  Late Cretaceous 35
  Late Devonian 25
  Ordovician 20
  sixth 50
megafauna, extinction of 31
Meganeura 26
meteorites 14, 15
methane 15, 30
Michel, Helen V. 35
microfossils 23
migration, human 44
Milankovitch cycles 30
Milankovitch, Milutin 30
milkweed 37
mitochondria 18
monotremes 38
Morganucodon 33
mosasaurs 34
Moschops 28
moss animals 20
moths
  hawk 36–7
  peppered 48
mutations 11, 12
mycorrhizae 24

N

natural selection 8, 9, 10–13, 37, 42, 48
nautiloids 20
Neanderthals 45
nectar 35, 36, 37
Neogene Period 40–1, 44–5, 51
nightingales 43
nitrogen 15
nothosaurs 32

O

oceans
  formation of 32
  Ordovician and Silurian 20–1
  trenches 9
On the Origin of Species (Darwin) 9
Onychonycteris 38
Opabinia 19
orchids 36–7
Ordovician Period 20
ossicles 29
ostracoderms 21
oxygen 15, 25, 27

P

Pakicetus 39
Palaeogene Period 38–9
Pangaea 16, 28, 29, 32
Paraceratherium 38
Parasaurolophus 34
parents 10, 11
Payeng, Jadav 51
peacocks 43
Permian Period 28–9
photosynthesis 15, 18, 25, 27
Pikaia 19
placoderms 24
plants
  first 18, 24
  first land 20
  flowering 34, 35, 36–7, 38, 39
  photosynthesis 15
  selective breeding 46
  spores and seeds 25
  vascular 21
plesiosaurs 34
Pneumodesmus newmanii 20
polar regions 39, 49
pollen 23, 35, 36
pollinators 36–7
pollution 48
populations 10, 11
primates 39
Proconsul 41
Procynosuchus 29
prokaryotes 18
Protaxites 20
Proterozoic Eon 18, 19
pterosaurs 34
Pulmonoscorpius 27

Q

Quaternary Period 16, 44–9, 51

R

radioactive elements 23
rainfall 32, 35
rainforests 6, 17, 51
ray-finned fish 24
reptiles 28, 32
  flying 34
  marine 32, 34
rock, dating 23
Romer, Alfred Sherwood 27

S

Şahin, Uğur 49
Sahni, Birbal 29
sauropods 33
Scutosaurus 28
sea scorpions 21
seed dispersal 35
seeds 25, 29, 36
selective breeding 46, 47
settlements 47
sexual selection 43
sharks, spiny 24
silk 47
Silk Road 47
Silurian Period 20, 21, 24
Smilodectes 39
song, bird 43
species
  changes over time 9, 10
  classification of 53
  coevolution 36–7
  isolation 13, 17, 42
spores 25
Stegosaurus 33
stromatolites 15
sugar 15
sunlight 15
supercontinents 16, 17
swamps 24, 26–7
synapsids 28, 29

T

tectonic plates 16, 17, 39
Thunberg, Greta 51
tool making 44, 45
tortoises, giant 17
trace fossils 22
trade 47
transport, plants 21
tree of life 52–3
trees
  first 25
  planting 50, 51
Triassic Period 16, 32, 38
Triceratops 34
trilobites 19
trunks, tree 25
Türeci, Özlem 49
Tyrannosaurus rex 34, 53

V

vaccinations 49
variation 10, 11, 12, 42
vents, deep ocean 14
vertebrates 24, 25, 38
  land-dwelling 26, 27
viruses 49
volcanoes 16, 29, 30, 32
voltziales 29
Vorobyeva, Emilia Ivanovna 25

W

Wallace, Alfred Russel 8–9, 10, 15, 36, 43
Wallace Line 9
warm-blooded animals 38
water 14
water vapour 15, 35
weather, extreme 49
Wegener, Alfred 16
whales 39

SELECTED SOURCES

The research process for this book was multi-layered and the authors used a wide range of reliable sources for each topic. In addition, experts have reviewed every topic for accuracy. The result is that many sources were used – more than is possible to share here. Below is a sample of the authors' sources.

General sources

American Museum of Natural History, New York www.amnh.org

Britannica Online Encyclopaedia. www.britannica.com

Benton, Michael J. *Vertebrate Palaeontology*. (Chichester, UK; Wiley Blackwell, 2015)

Berta, Annalisa and Susan Turner. *Rebels, scholars, explorers: women in vertebrate paleontology*. (Baltimore, MD; Johns Hopkins University Press, 2020)

Darwin, Charles. *On the origin of species*. (London, UK; John Murray 1859)

Kemp, Tom S. *The Origin and Evolution of Mammals*. (Oxford, UK; Oxford University Press, 2004)

Natural History Museum, London www.nhm.ac.uk/discover.html

Stanley, Steven M., and John A. Luczaj. *Earth System History*. (New York; W. H. Freeman, 2015)

Taylor, Thomas N., Edith L. Taylor and Michael Krings. *Paleobotany, the biology and evolution of fossil plants*. (Amsterdam, Netherlands; Academic Press, 2009)

TrowelBlazers www.trowelblazers.com/

Willis, Kathy J. and Jennifer C. McElwain. *The Evolution of Plants*. (Oxford, UK; Oxford University Press, 2013)

Pages 8–9: Darwin and Wallace

Berry, R.J. 'Standing on the shoulders of giants: Wollaston, Wallace, Darwin, Hooker and more'. In: Perez, V. & C. Ramon (eds.) *Islands and Evolution*. (Minorca: Institut Menorquí d'Estudis, 2010), pp. 27–58

Wallace, Alfred Russel. 'On the physical geography of the Malay Archipelago', *Royal Geographical Society* 7: 205–212 (1863)

Pages 10–11: Natural Selection

Barbehenn, Raymond V. and Peter C. Constabel. 'Tannins in plant-herbivore interactions', *Phytochemistry* 72: 1551–1565 (2011)

Davison, Angus, Hannah J. Jackson, Ellis W. Murphy and Tom Reader. 'Discrete or indiscrete? Redefining the colour polymorphism of the land snail *Cepaea nemoralis*', *Heredity* 123: 162–175 (2019)

Pages 14–15: How It All Began

Blaustein, Richard. 'The Great Oxidation Event: Evolving understandings of how oxygenic life on Earth began', *BioScience* 66.3 189–195 (2016)

Nutman, Allen Phillip, Vickie C. Bennett, Clark R. Friend, Martin J. Van Kranendonk and Allan R. Chivas. 'Rapid emergence of life shown by discovery of 3,700-million-year-old microbial structures', *Nature* 537: 535–538 (2016)

Piani, Laurette and Guillaume Paris. 'Why is there water on Earth?' theconversation.com/why-is-there-water-on-earth-153931

Pages 16–17 Planet Earth Rocks!

Frazier, Jack 'The Galapagos: Island home of giant tortoises'. In: Gibbs, James P., Cayot, Linda J., and Washington Tapia Aguilera (eds), *Galapagos Giant Tortoises*, pp. 1–22 (London, UK, Academic Press, 2021)

Scotese, Christopher R., 'Paleomap Project', www.scotese.com/earth.htm

Kooyman, Robert M. et al. 'Paleo-Antarctic rainforest into the modern old world tropics: the rich past and threatened future of the 'southern wet forest survivors', American Journal of Botany 101: 2121–2135

Pages 18–19: Life Fills the Seas

Darroch, Simon A. F., Emily F. Smith, Marc Laflamme and Douglas H Erwin. 'Ediacaran Extinction and Cambrian Explosion', *Trends in Ecology & Evolution* 33: 653–663 (2018)

Keeling, Patrick J. 'The endosymbiotic origin, diversification and fate of plastids', *Philosophical Transactions of the Royal Society* B 365: 729–748 (2010)

'The Cambrian Explosion' burgess-shale.rom.on.ca/en/index.php

Pages 20–21: Life Finds a New Home

Boyce, C. Kevin, Carol L. Hotton, Marilyn L. Fogel, George D. Cody, Robert M. Hazen, Andrew H. Knoll and Francis M. Hueber. 'Devonian landscape heterogenetiy recorded by a giant fungus', *Geology* 35: 399–402 (2007)

Suarez, Stephanie E., Michael E. Brookfield, Elizabeth J. Catlos and Daniel F. Stöckli. 'A U-Pb zircon age constraint on the oldest-recorded air-breathing land animal', *PLoS ONE* 12: e0179262 (2017)

Morris, Jennifer L., Mark N. Puttick, James W. Clark, Dianne Edwards, Paul Kenrick, Silvia Pressel, Charles H. Wellman, Ziheng Yang, Harald Schneider and Philip C. J. Donoghue. 'The timescale of early land plant evolution', *Proceedings of the National Academy of Science USA*, 115: E2274–E2283 (2018)

Pages 22–23: Fantastic Fossils

'Geologic age dating explained' www.acs.org/pressroom/reactions/library/how-do-we-know-the-age-of-the-earth.html

Pages 24–25: Animals Find Their Feet

Barash, Max S. 'Causes of the Great Mass Extinction of Marine Organisms in the Late Devonian,' *Coeanology* 56: 863–875 (2016)

Cloutier, Richard, Alice M. Clement, Michael S. Y. Lee, Roxanne Noël, Isabelle Béchard, Vincent Roy and John A. Long. '*Elpistostege* and the origin of the vertebrate hand', *Nature* 579: 549–554 (2020)

Taylor, Thomas N., Winfried Remy, Hagen Hass and Hans Kerp. 'Fossil arbuscular mycorrhizae from the Early Devonian', *Mycologia* 87: 560–573 (1995)

Pages 26–27: Giants From the Swamps

Rasnitsyn, Alexandr P. and Donald L. J. Quicke, eds. *History of Insects*. (New York; Kluwer Academic Publishers, 2002)

Smithson, Timothy R., Stanley P. Wood, John E. A. Marschall and Jennifer A. Clack. 'Earliest Carboniferous tetrapod and arthropod faunas from Scotland populate Romer's Gap', *Proceedings of the National Academy of Science USA* 109: 4532–4537 (2012)

Verberk, Wilco C. E. P. and David T. Bilton. 'Can Oxygen set thermal limits in an Insect and drive gigantism?' *PLoS ONE* 6: e22610 (2011)

Pages 28–29: Icehouse to Hothouse

Bajdek, Piotr, Martin Qvarnström, Krzysztof Owocki, Tomasz Sulej, Andrey G. Sennikov, Valeriy K. Golubev and Grzegorz Niedźwiedzki. 'Microbiota and food residues including possible evidence of pre-mammalian hair in Upper Permian coprolites from Russia', *Lethaia* 49: 455–477 (2016)

Daley, Jim. 'Now hear this: new fossils reveal early ear-bone evolution', www.scientificamerican.com/article/now-hear-this-new-fossils-reveal-early-ear-bone-evolution/

Ruta, Marcello, Jennifer Botha-Brink, Stephen A. Mitchell and Michael J. Benton. 'The radiation of cynodonts and the ground plan of mammalian morphological diversity', *Proceedings of the Royal Society B* 280: 20131865 (2013)

Pages 30–31: The Causes of Climate Change

Buis, Alan. 'Milankovitch (Orbital) Cycles and their role in Earth's climate', climate.nasa.gov/news/2948/milankovitch-orbital-cycles-and-their-role-in-earths-climate/

Allmon, Warren D., Trisha A. Smrecak and Robert M Ross. *Climate Change, Past, Present and Future – A Very Short Guide*. (Ithaca, NY; Paleontological Research Institution: 2010)

Mann, Daniel H., Pamela Groves, Richard E., Benjamin V Gaglioti, Michael L. Kunz and Beth Shapiro. 'Life and extinction of megafauna in the ice-age Arctic', *Proceedings of the National academy of Sciences USA* 112: 14301–14306

Pages 32–33: Dinosaurs in Charge

Gore, Rick. 'The rise of mammals', www.nationalgeographic.com/science/article/rise-mammals

'When is a dinosaur not a dinosaur?' www.theguardian.com/science/2009/feb/07/dinosaurs-science-fossils-zoology

Pickrell, John. 'How the earliest mammals thrived alongside dinosaurs', *Nature* 574, 468–472 (2019)

Pages 34–35: *T. rex* and the Rise of Flowers

Friis, Else Marie, Peter R. Crane and Kaj Raunsgaard Pedersen. *Early flowers and angiosperm evolution*. (Cambridge, UK; Cambridge University Press, 2011)

Boyce, C. Kevin, Jung-Eun Lee, Taylor S. Feild, Tim J. Brodribb and Maciej A. Zwieniecki. 'Angiosperms helped put the rain in the rainforests: the impact of plant physiological evolution on tropical biodiversity', *Annals of the Missouri Botanical Garden* 97: 527–540 (2010)

Mark P. Witton. '*Pteranodon* and beyond: the history of giant pterosaurs from 1870', *Geological Society, London, Special Publications* 343: 13–323 (2010)

Pages 36–37: Evolving Together

Agrawal, Anurag A. *Monarchs and Milkweed. A migrating butterfly, a poisonous plant, and their remarkable story of coevolution* (Princeton, NJ; Princeton University Press, 2017)

Minet, Joël, Patrick Basquin, Jean Haxaire, David C. Lees and Rodolphe Rougerie. 'A new taxonomic status for Darwin's 'predicted' pollinator: *Xanthopan praedicta* stat. nov.', Antenor 8: 69–86 (2021)

Pages 38–39: The Age of Mammals

Collinson, Margaret E. and Jerry J. Hooker. 'Paleogene vegetation of Eurasia: framework for mammalian faunas', Deinsea 10: 41–83 (2003)

Padian, Kevin and Brian Swartz. 'The evolution of whales', https://evolution.berkeley.edu/what-are-evograms/the-evolution-of-whales/

Storch, G., Burkart Engesser and Matthias Wuttke. 'Oldest fossil record of gliding in rodents', *Nature* 379: 439–441 (1996)

Pages 40–41: Grasslands and Grazers

Harrison, Terry. *Proconsul. The international Encyclopedia of Primatology*, Vol. III, Fuentes, Agustín (ed.), (John Wiley & Sons, 2017)

Yin, Steph, 'How horses got their hooves', www.nytimes.com/2017/08/28/science/horses-hooves-evolution.html

Maguire, Kaitlin Clare and Alycia L. Stigall. 'Paleobiogeography of Miocene Equinae of North America: a phylogenetic biogeographic analysis of the relative roles of climate, vicariance, and dispersal', *Palaeogeography, Palaeoclimatology, Palaeoecology* 267: 1175–184 (2008)

Pages 42–43: The Success of Birds

Brennan, P. 'Sexual Selection', *Nature Education Knowledge* 3 (10): 79 (2010)

Bartsch, Conny, Michael Weiss, and Silke Kipper. 'Multiple song features are related to paternal effort in common nightingales', *BMC Evolutionary Biology* 15 (115) (2015)

Borgia, Gerald, Ingrid M. Kaatz and Richard Condit 'Flower choice and bower decoration in the satin bowerbird *Ptilonorhynchus violaceus*: a test of hypotheses for the evolution of male display', *Animal Behaviour*, Volume 35, Issue 4, pp. 1129–1139. (1987)

Pages 44–45: Evolution of Humans

Harmand, Sonia et al. '3.3-million-year-old stone tools from Lomekwi 3, West Turkana, Kenya', Nature 521, 310–315 (2015)

Williams, Blythe A., Richard F. Kay, Christopher Kirk E. 'New perspectives on anthropoid origins', Proceedings of the National academy of Sciences USA 107: 4797–4804 (2009)

Smithsonian National Museum of Natural History, 'What does it mean to be human?' humanorigins.si.edu

Pages 46–47: Humans Change Their World

Ahmad, Hafiz Ishfaq, Muhammad Jamil Ahmad, Farwa Jabbir, Sunny Ahmar, Nisar Ahmad, Abdelmotaleb A. Elokil and Jinping Chen. 'The Domestication Makeup: Evolution, Survival, and Challenges', *Frontiers in Ecololgy and Evolution* 8: 103 (2020)

Sullivan, Alexis P., Douglas W. Bird and George H. Perry. 'Human behaviour as a long-term ecological driver of non-human evolution', *Nature Ecology & Evolution* 1, 0065 (2017)

Marshall, Michael. 'Humans may have domesticated dogs by accident by sharing excess meat', www.newscientist.com/article/2264329-humans-may-have-domesticated-dogs-by-accident-by-sharing-excess-meat/

Pages 48–49: Human-Made

Wadgymar, Susana M., Rachel MacTavish and Jill T. Anderson, 'Evolutionary consequences of climate change' In: Jacqueline E. Mohan (ed.), *Ecosystem Consequences of Soil Warming*, Pages 29–59 (London, UK; Academic Press, 2019)

Winchell, Kristin M., Graham R. Reynolds, Sofia R. Prado-Irwin, Alberto R. Puente-Rolón, Liam J. Revell. 'Phenotypic shifts in urban areas in the tropical lizard *Anolis cristatellus*', *Evolution* 70: 1009–1022 (2016)

Hurley, C. and S. Montgomery. 'Peppered moths and Melanism', Darwin 2009 Christ's College. Cambridge, UK (2009)

Pages 50–51: The Future

'Young champions of the Earth – Fatema Alzelzela' www.unep.org/youngchampions/bio/2020/west-asia/fatemah-alzelzela

Foggin, Sophie. 'Helena Gualinga is a voice for indigenous communities in the fight against climate change' latinamericareports.com/helena-gualinga-voice-indigenous-communities-fight-climate-change/4192/

'Wangari Maathai' www.greenbeltmovement.org/wangari-maathai/biography

Zoeller, Chezza. 'Reforestation Hero: Jadav Payeng' www.oneearth.org/reforestation-hero-jadav-payeng/

Pages 52–53: Tree of Life

'Dinosaurs in the Tree of Life' www.geol.umd.edu/~tholtz/H259C/lectures/259Cvertebrates.html

Hidenori Nishihara, Masami Hasegawa and Norihiro Okada. '*Pegasoferae*, an unexpected mammalian clade revealed by tracking ancient retroposon insertions', *Proceedings of the National Academy of Sciences USA* 103: 9929–9934 (2006)

Leubner, Fanny, Monika Endres and Matthias Mau. *Der Stammbaum der Tiere* (Göttingen, Germany; Planet Poster Editions 2018)

NATURAL HISTORY COLLECTIONS

In the past, scientific research and collections of living things were often made without discussion with or regard for local people and cultures. In 1992, an international framework was put in place to protect nature, respect people and share knowledge. The Museum für Naturkunde Berlin and the Natural History Museum, London, both work to that framework and have built partnerships with scientists from all around the world. Today, science is a team effort.

ACKNOWLEDGEMENTS

This book is like an expedition through Earth's history and the evolution of life. As with all expeditions, it takes a team of people, often experts in different fields, who help along the way. We could not have written this book without the brilliant advice from our research colleagues, from the Museum für Naturkunde Berlin (MfN), in Germany and beyond. We would like to thank:

Alexander R. Schmidt (University of Göttingen, Germany), Andrea Deneau (Linnean Society of London, UK), Christina Beimforde (University of Göttingen, Germany), Daniela Schwarz (MfN), Dieter Korn (MfN), Faysal Bibi (MfN), Florian Witzmann (MfN), Frieder Mayer (MfN), Harald Schneider (Xishuangbanna Tropical Botanical Garden, Yunnan, China), Helen Gries (Vorderasiatisches Museum Berlin, Germany), James T. Costa (Western Carolina University, USA), Jan-Peter Duda (University of Göttingen, Germany), Janis Antonovics (University of Virginia, USA), Johannes Vogel (MfN), Jörg Fröbisch (MfN), Lauren Sumner-Rooney (MfN), Leyla J. Seyfullah (University of Vienna, Austria), Ludwig Luthardt (MfN), Mark-Oliver Rödel (MfN), Mary Gibby (Royal Botanic Garden Edinburgh, UK), Michael Ohl (MfN), Mirjam Knörnschild (MfN), Mozes Blom (MfN), Nicholas J. Conard (University of Tübingen, Germany), Peter Wilf (Pennsylvania State University, USA), Robert Kooyman (Macquarie University Sydney, Australia), Sandra Knapp (Natural History Museum, London, UK), Shigeru Kuratani (Kobe University, Japan), Stephan Schultka (MfN), Sylke Frahnert (MfN), Thomas Kruijer (Lawrence Livermore National Laboratory, USA), Washington Tapia Aguilera (Parque Nacional Galápagos, Ecuador) and Yara Haridy (University of Chicago, USA). We would also like to thank Nora Lentge-Maaß (MfN), Hans Lentge and their daughter Ida Lentge for their inspiring research project on grove snails, which they undertook especially for this book.

This book has been undertaken in collaboration with the Natural History Museum, London, and we would like to thank Colin Ziegler and the many members of staff who have supported our journey.

Finally we would like to thank Christopher Lloyd and What on Earth Books, especially Katy Lennon for her patient advice and editorial skills, Nell Wood for creating the wonderful designs and page layouts and Nancy Feresten for all the inspiring discussions. We would also like to thank Olga Baumert for bringing our text to life with her lovely illustrations. We are grateful to Stephen M. Tomecek for his excellent science editing and fact-checking.

Sarah would like to thank Johannes, Leo and Jos for all their love and patience. Eva's grateful thanks go to Hamid for his encouragement, love and support throughout.

MEET THE AUTHORS

DR SARAH DARWIN

I originally trained as an artist and then as a scientist. I specialised in plant sciences, which is known as botany. Over several years, I spent months at a time living and working in the Galápagos Islands and studying the Galápagos tomatoes. More recently, I have been part of a project in Berlin studying nightingales – they are shy little birds with an amazing song. Charles Darwin is my great-great grandfather. When I was a child, I didn't understand the significance of his work. But now I know how truly ground-breaking his studies were. I was very excited to write this book to share these discoveries with you, too! It is so important to remember that humans are part of nature and not above it. This is a relationship that needs to be loved and cherished.

DR EVA-MARIA SADOWSKI

I am a palaeobotanist, which means that I research plants that lived a long time ago. I mainly study plant remains that are enclosed in amber. I find it fascinating how plants that have been preserved in amber can look as fresh today as when they fell off the tree millions of years ago. Many of these plant fossils look different from their living relatives today, and this helps us to understand how plants have evolved and changed throughout time. Like amber, this book provides us with windows into Earth's past environments. We hope that it will help you to build a picture of how our rich and exciting world evolved. Understanding the history of life on Earth helps us to understand the world we live in today – how it functions and how it might change in the future. This understanding ensures that we can be part of the decisions that affect the complex system of life on Earth.

Sarah and Eva-Maria are both scientific researchers at Berlin's Natural History Museum – Museum für Naturkunde Berlin, Leibniz Institute for Evolution and Biodiversity Science in Germany.

Photo credits: Photo of Sarah taken by Hans Fels, photo of Eva taken by Hwa Ja Götz, MfN

What on Earth Books is an imprint of What on Earth Publishing
The Black Barn, Wickhurst Farm, Leigh, Tonbridge, Kent, UK, TN11 8PS
30 Ridge Road Unit B, Greenbelt, Maryland, 20770, United States

First published in the United Kingdom in 2023
Published in association with the Natural History Museum, London

Written by Sarah Darwin and Eva-Maria Sadowski
Illustrated by Olga Baumert
Designed by Nell Wood

Sarah Darwin and Eva-Maria Sadowski have asserted their right to be identified as authors of this work and Olga Baumert has asserted her right to be identified as illustrator under the Copyright, Designs and Patents Act 1988.

Staff for this book: Publisher, Nancy Feresten; Senior Editor, Katy Lennon; Art Director, Andy Forshaw; Senior Designer, Nell Wood; Production Manager, Lauren Fulbright.

Consultants: Stephen M. Tomecek and Paul D. Taylor

With thanks to the Museum für Naturkunde Berlin (MfN) – Leibniz Institute for Evolution and Biodiversity Science. The MfN is an integrated research museum within the Leibniz Association and is situated in the centre of Berlin, Germany. As a research museum and innovative communication platform, the MfN wants to engage in and influence the scientific and societal discourse about the future of our planet. It is one of the most important research institutions worldwide on biological and geological evolution, biodiversity, collection development and public engagement. The MfN's work is structured around three programs: Dynamic Nature, Collection Future and Society and Nature. The MfN collection comprises some 30 million objects and the exhibitions and public programs are enjoyed by one million visitors and participants each year. For more information please visit us at: **www.museumfuernaturkunde.berlin/en**

A CIP catalogue record for this book is available from the British Library

ISBN: 978-93-5954-795-4

Published and Distributed in India by
Scholastic India Pvt. Ltd.

This Reprint Edition: August, 2024

Printed in India at Polykam Offset New Delhi 110028